A New Owner's
Guide to
PEMBROKE
WELSH CORGIS

JG-172

T.F.H. Publications, Inc.
One TFH Plaza
Third and Union Avenues
Neptune City, NJ 07753

This book has been published with the intent to provide accurate and authoritative information in regard to the subject matter within. While every precaution has been taken in preparation of this book, the publisher and author assume no responsibility for errors or omissions. Neither is any liability assumed for damages resulting from the use of the information herein.

ISBN 0-7938-2821-X

www.tfh.com

A NEW OWNER'S GUIDE TO
PEMBROKE
WELSH CORGIS

SUSAN M. EWING

Contents

2004 Edition

Children and Corgis usually become friends easily.

Corgis excel at agility.

Chew toys help to keep your Corgi's teeth clean.

Your Corgi needs time outside to exercise.

Traveling should be fun for both you and your Corgis.

His adorable appearance makes the Pembroke Welsh Corgi a favorite among dog fanciers.

HISTORY of the Pembroke Welsh Corgi

The history of the Pembroke Welsh Corgi, like the history of all dog breeds, started long before there were any known specific breeds at all. Most dog historians only go back 10,000 to 14,000 years, to the first evidence that there was a relationship between canines and men. They generally agree that the northern wolf is behind many of the so-called northern breeds, as well as the spitz family, including the Pembroke Welsh Corgi.

While the Pembroke Welsh Corgi may not be as old as some of the breeds depicted in ancient Egyptian artwork, the breed is definitely not new. It has been around for about 1,000 years. The name "Corgi" is from "Cur-gi," meaning "dwarf dog." This name was even mentioned in the 10th century laws of Wales.

How the breed evolved is not known for sure. There are many different opinions, and several breeds are suggested as having contributed to the Pembroke Welsh Corgi we know today.

W. Lloyd-Thomas, writing in an article that appeared in *Pure-Bred Dogs—American Kennel Gazette* in 1935, said, "...the Pembroke

The origin of the Pembroke Welsh Corgi is not exactly known. W. Lloyd-Thomas believed, as do many Pembroke fanciers, that the Pembroke Welsh Corgi is descended from members of the larger spitz family.

and Cardigan Welsh Corgi originated as two entirely separate and unrelated breeds, the Pembroke being a member of the large spitz family and the Cardigan evolving from the Dachshund or Tekel class. Members of the spitz family, such as the Schipperke, the Pomeranian, the Keeshond and the Samoyed, are characterized by prick ears, a pointed muzzle, and (in most) a curly tail. The Tekel group, which includes the Dachshund and the Basset Hound, are essentially long-bodied, deep-chested, short-legged dogs, heavier in muzzle than typical Spitz types."

Lloyd-Thomas maintained that the Cardigan breed influenced the breed that was to become the Pembroke, but the traffic in puppies never flowed the other way, and changes in the original Cardigan were a result of mixing with other breeds, not the Pembroke: "The Cardigan Corgi's gradual refinement and somewhat diminished size from that of the original Corgi, along with a change of ear carriage from a drooping ear to an erect, slightly hooded ear, plus changes in coat quality, all supposedly were brought about by the influence of breeds other than the Pembroke Corgi..."

Although the two breeds of Corgi are definitely different, it doesn't seem likely that the two breeds were not bred together at times and that certain traits were shared. As Charles Lister-Kaye notes in his book, *The Popular Welsh Corgi,* both Pembroke and Cardigan Welsh Corgis were shown together between 1925 and 1934, before the Kennel Club recognized them as separate breeds.

Breeds that may have contributed to the modern-day Corgi include the Lundehund, the Swedish Vallhund, the Buhund, the Finnehund (which may be the Finnish Lapphund, Swedish Lapphund, or the Vallhund), the Welsh Heeler, and whatever dogs the Flemish weavers brought with them, probably Schipperke or Pomeranian-type dogs. With the exception of the Welsh Heeler, all of these dogs have spitz characteristics.

David Hancock describes the two breeds of Corgis in *Old Farm Dogs.* "The Welsh Heeler is perpetuated in the Pembrokeshire and Cardiganshire Corgis, originally more like leggy Dachshunds and often with drop ears, unlike the prick-eared dogs of today. The Pembrokeshire dog is more like the spitz breeds of northern Europe... The Cardiganshire Corgi is less spitz-like, with a full tail, and resembles a miniature version of the Welsh Hillman."

The Pembroke Welsh Corgi has captured the hearts of owners in homes around the world.

For an idea of the other dogs that may have entered the mix, *The Atlas of Dog Breeds of the World*, by Bonnie Wilcox and Chris Walkowicz, gives some telling descriptions.

The Lundehund of Norway weighs only about 14 pounds and measures 12 1/2 to 14 1/2 inches tall. These dogs are brown with black tipping on each hair and some white markings. They have prick ears and are double jointed as well as having extra toes to facilitate rock climbing as they hunt for puffins. Their markings and ears are very similar to those of a Pembroke Welsh Corgi, although Corgis are not known to have extra toes. The Corgi of today is heavier, but with some other breeds thrown in, there's no way to rule out a dash of Lundehund blood.

The Buhund is another Norwegian breed that may also have contributed to the Corgi. It stands 17-18 inches tall, weighs 26-40 pounds, and was originally a herding dog. They come in wheaten, black, and sable and may have white markings and/or a black mask. That certainly sounds like a Corgi!

The Swedish Vallhund weighs 20-32 pounds and stands 13 to 16 inches high. This dog looks a lot like a Corgi, but there seems to be a question as to whether the Vallhund traveled to Wales or the Corgi traveled to Sweden. Again, we'll never know.

The Lapphund is taller yet, at 18 to 20 inches, and weighs closer to 45 pounds, but maybe the breed's longer fur contributed to the "fluffy" gene in Corgis.

Whatever the mix in a Corgi, the result is an energetic, intelligent dog. Because of his size, he didn't require much food or space on the early Welsh farms but could make himself useful in many areas. Traditionally, Pembroke Welsh Corgis were used to move stock from one place to another, frequently to market, while Cardigan Welsh Corgis were used to scatter stock over the common grazing ground and then round it up again at night. Although known as a herding dog, especially when it came to cattle and geese, the Pembroke Welsh Corgi was also useful as a ratter in the barn and could even retrieve fallen game. Today, that energetic little dog makes a wonderful family pet, and he's also an eager partner in whatever activity his owner might enjoy, whether it's fetching a stick or ball, herding, competing in obedience, agility, tracking, or conformation.

The more recent history of the Corgi is easier to follow. The first record of a Corgi being shown in England was in 1925, the same

A day romping in the snow will make any Pembroke Welsh Corgi happy.

year the Welsh Corgi Club was formed. In the beginning, both types of Corgi were classified as one breed, but by 1934, the Kennel Club officially recognized the Pembroke and Cardigan Corgis as separate breeds.

It may have helped the popularity of the Pembroke Welsh Corgi that Britain's royal family took an interest in the breed. In 1933, the Duke of York, who would become King George VI, bought a Pembroke Welsh Corgi for his two daughters, Elizabeth and Margaret. The puppy came from Thelma Gray of Rozavel Kennel, and his registered name was Rozavel Golden Eagle. While Gray had the puppy for housetraining, she began calling him "The Duke" because of his rather regal, self-assured attitude, and this name led to "Dookie." Dookie he remained, and Rozavel Lady Jane soon joined him in the royal household. Jane was bred and her puppies were born on Christmas Eve; the royal family kept two of her puppies, Crackers and Carol. In 1944, on her eighteenth birthday, Elizabeth II received a Corgi named Susan, and she has owned descendents of Susan ever since.

Susan is buried at Sandringham, as is her daughter, Sugar, and a granddaughter, Heather. It is customary for the Queen's dogs to be buried at whatever house the Queen is living in at the time of their deaths. Many are buried at Windsor Castle. The Queen has owned more than 30 Corgis during her reign, as well as eight Dorgis, crosses between one of her Corgis and a longhaired miniature Dachshund owned by Princess Margaret. As of June 2003, the Queen owned Corgis named Pharos, Emma, and Linnet, as well as three that had belonged to the late Queen Mother, Rush, Minnie, and Monty. She also owns three Dorgis, Brandy, Cider, and Berry.

On this side of the Atlantic, Little Madam became the first Pembroke Welsh Corgi registered with the American Kennel Club in 1934. Mrs. Lewis Roesler of Massachusetts had brought her to this country in 1933, and Little Madam was registered as simply a Welsh Corgi. By 1935, the two separate breeds, Cardigan and Pembroke, were acknowledged with the registration of Cardigan Welsh Corgi Blodwen of Robinscroft.

In 1936, The Pembroke Welsh Corgi Club of America (PWCCA) was founded and held its first specialty show in conjunction with the Morris and Essex show in New Jersey. The total number of Pembroke Welsh Corgis registered at that time was 33, and the Morris and Essex Show drew seven. This contrasts quite sharply with 2002, when 9,921 Corgis were registered in that year, and almost 400 Corgis were entered in the national specialty. With the exception of the war years of 1943, 1944, and 1945, the PWCCA has held a national specialty every year and held two in 1960 and 1963. The PWCCA publishes a quarterly newsletter and offers special awards each year for top-ranking Corgis. The Club also publishes and sells an illustrated standard of the Pembroke Welsh Corgi, which is very useful in understanding the points covered by the official standard.

Look at old pictures of the Pembroke Welsh Corgi and you'll see that the breed is still evolving. The older Corgis had longer legs, shorter, closer coats, and weighed less. Today, Corgis are rarely considered for use in retrieving fallen game, and people think of terriers and not Corgis when they think of ridding a barn of vermin. The one thing that hasn't changed is the Corgi's intelligence, curiosity, and independent nature. The Corgi can be a challenge, but that challenge is part of his charm.

CHARACTERISTICS of the Pembroke Welsh Corgi

All puppies, no matter what the breed, are adorable. It's hard to resist a puppy when he crawls into your lap and licks your chin. A puppy is so warm, cuddly, and cute that it's hard to remember why a puppy might not be a good idea.

Presumably, if you're at the stage where a puppy is crawling into your lap, you've done some homework and are seriously looking for an addition to your family. If you aren't already looking, take a minute to think about what having a puppy means. Do all the members of the family want a dog? If you have children, their vote is probably yes. They may even say they will take care of the dog. They may even mean it, but depending on their age, they may not be able to do everything for the dog, and they may eventually ignore the unpleasant aspects of dog care or lose interest after the novelty has worn off. It's up to the adults in a family to commit to the care of the dog for his lifetime, which in the case of a Corgi is usually 12 to 14 years. If the person who will be the primary caregiver doesn't really want a

There are many places for you to get your Corgi. Carefully examine any dog before you make your final selection.

All Pembroke pups are cute. Take your time to get the right dog for you and your family.

dog, then a dog is not a good idea. Maybe a goldfish or two would be better.

If the adults in the family want a dog and are willing to take care of his needs—from food and water to housetraining and necessary visits to the veterinarian, not to mention playtime and exercise— then it's time to choose a breed that everyone will enjoy. One of the advantages to choosing a purebred is that you know ahead of time what size the dog will be as an adult or whether he will have long or short hair. Is the breed known for curling up in your lap or for eagerly retrieving ducks from icy water?

Another advantage to choosing a purebred is the breeder. Find a good breeder and you'll have an invaluable source of help and information during your pet's life. A reputable breeder will give you both the pros and cons of living with a particular breed. He or she will tell you about possible health problems and about the temperament of his or her line. You'll also be able to see some adult dogs from that line, which will give you an even better idea of what your puppy will be like as an adult. There are certain basic traits that you'll find in all Corgis, but within the breed, there is still a wide range of personalities. You'll find a list of breeders at the AKC website, as well as at the national club's site.

If it's true that all puppies are adorable, then Corgi puppies are extra adorable. It's hard to resist these charming little canines with their cute, furry, tailless rears and their ears that are trying hard to stay upright but may flop over without warning, especially when they are teething.

However, before you meet a puppy and fall in love, consider what living with a Corgi will be like. For starters, there's the question of coat. The good news is that Corgis don't require much fancy grooming. You won't need to make a standing appointment with your local groomer to keep your Corgi's coat in shape. The bad news is that Corgis have a thick double coat. This coat keeps them warm and dry, but it also means that they shed lightly all the time and very heavily twice a year. Many people like the idea of a dog but not the idea of a lot of hair. With a Corgi, you will need to brush

Pembroke Welsh Corgis are intelligent dogs. Sometimes owning an intelligent dog means more work for its owner.

out all that dead undercoat twice a year, and regular grooming the rest of the year really is necessary. If you don't want dog hairs on your rug, furniture, clothes, and in little "dust bunny" clumps under your bed, you'd better find another breed.

The official standard for the Pembroke Welsh Corgi describes the Corgi as having a bold but kindly outlook, with an intelligent and interested expression. The Corgi should never be shy or vicious. That's a very compact statement and, while it's all true, it can be expanded upon. Corgis tend to combine both fearlessness and curiosity, which can get them into trouble. Most puppies have a certain blend of these characteristics, but Corgis carry these traits with them their entire lives. They enjoy exploring anything new and will eagerly pursue whatever interests them, which is why a fenced-in yard is so important.

And, although the idea of owning an intelligent dog sounds good, sometimes that intelligence means extra work for the owner. Corgis can often figure out solutions to problems that you might have wished they hadn't—such as opening the refrigerator door. Corgis learn quickly. If you don't want them on the furniture or on your bed, keep them on the floor. Don't let that cute little puppy

Some Corgis are very quiet and don't want to herd, play, fetch, or even bark.

By properly training your Corgi from the time he enters your home, you'll have a wonderful addition to your family.

sleep at the foot of the bed or curl up on the couch next to you if you won't want the adult doing the same thing. Give a Corgi an inch and he will definitely take the proverbial mile. If you intend to let your adult sleep with you, fine. But if not, don't allow the behavior as a pup.

Corgis are personality plus. They are always ready to join in whatever fun their human family may suggest. Most Corgis will retrieve a ball or toy for far longer than the human partner will want to continue. Their boldness and curiosity make them a natural on the agility course. Their intelligence makes them quick learners of the obedience routine. This intelligence can work against you, though. Corgis may become bored with the way a particular obedience exercise is done. They may add their own twist to it. One of my Corgis quickly learned that the command that followed "front" was "heel". When I called her, then, instead of coming straight at me and sitting in front of me, she skipped that part and ran around me into the heel position. Lots of treats convinced her that sitting in front first was a good idea.

It's not unusual for a Corgi to anticipate the next step in any series of events. One of my male Corgis knew just when we were going to go for a walk. No, not when I picked up the lead or put on my coat or got a supply of bags, but when I put on my shoes.

Because Corgis are fearless, it's up to you to protect them from themselves. Corgis are short, but they won't hesitate to launch themselves from your bed or the couch or even a grooming table. If they are up on a relatively high surface, help them to the ground. Corgis are not as susceptible to back injuries as longer dogs, such as the Dachshund, but constantly jumping down from high places can lead to back and shoulder injuries. If you enjoy having your Corgi with you on a high bed or couch, consider building or buying a doggy ramp.

Corgis aren't usually afraid of bigger dogs, even when they should be. Males, especially, may be aggressive toward other dogs. Be aware of this attitude and prevent confrontations between your Corgi and other dogs. Socialization when your dog is young can help with this problem.

The Corgi is a herding breed. Just because you don't have any cattle, sheep, or ducks doesn't mean that your dog won't try to herd. Small children running through the yard may provoke a Corgi to chase them and nip at their heels. It's the Corgi's nature to chase and

Daily exercise is important in keeping your Pembroke Welsh Corgi healthy and happy.

nip at moving objects. This doesn't mean the dog is vicious, and the nips rarely turn into bites, but it can be scary to a child. Make sure your children and their friends understand this. Keep your Corgi inside if it's a problem. You can teach a Corgi not to nip, but it's like teaching a terrier not to dig. It takes a lot of work, and even then it may not be successful all the time.

If you have company, your Corgi may bark until everyone is seated and quiet. Corgis can be very bossy. They like to be in the center of the activity, and they like to know what's going on. Obedience training may not be necessary, but it is advisable. Even if you never want to compete in formal obedience trials, it's a good idea to teach your Corgi the basic commands. While you can learn how to do this from books, a good class will also help you to socialize your Corgi. Getting him used to other people and dogs is a must for a well-socialized dog.

Some Corgis are very quiet and don't seem to want to herd, play, fetch, or even bark at intruders, but it's not something to count on. Most Corgis love retrieving and most will try to herd at some time. Barking does vary considerably, but again, don't count on your Corgi being the strong, silent type. Corgis are excellent watchdogs, so if you want a quiet dog, you'd better look elsewhere. While the degree of barking may differ, Corgis will definitely let you know when someone is at the door or a strange car has driven up. If you can't stand the thought of a barking dog, you'd better get a different breed.

Physically, Corgis are short and should weigh less than 30 pounds. This means that you can pick them up if you have to, which can be an advantage when your dog is sick and can't jump into the car on his own for that trip to the veterinarian's. They are sturdy enough, though, to play with children and not get injured if the play should get a little rough. Their size makes them a bit less intimidating to both children and guests.

Your Corgi will need daily exercise and preferably a fenced yard. A loose Corgi is a lost Corgi. Their eager, happy approach to life means they like to see what's next door, what's down the block, what's over the hill. It's not recommended that you tie a Corgi out for long periods. That would certainly work for morning and evening trips to the yard, but then you'd need to include two or three brisk walks for exercise, as well as some indoor games. Even with a fenced yard, your Corgi will need some playtime; playtime

All exercise should be supervised. When you cannot supervise your dog, make sure he is in a fenced-in yard where he cannot escape

ensures that your dog receives enough exercise and is able to spend quality time with you. Corgis are very much "people" dogs. They need to be a part of the family, not shut away in their crates or left out in the yard.

At the same time, Corgis certainly don't need as much exercise as, say, a Border Collie or a Weimaraner. And if a day goes by without that long hike or a tiring game of fetch, the Corgi will not insist on an outing just when you want to sit down and relax.

Corgis are also chowhounds. They love to eat and can look very pathetic when you're having a snack and they're not. The amount of food a Corgi will need will depend on how active he is, so you may need to do a bit of adjusting before you discover the right amount of food. Once you do, try to stick with that amount. Overweight animals can suffer poor health just like overweight humans. They can develop joint problems, heart disease, and diabetes. The occasional bit of cheese or leftover scrambled egg won't kill your Corgi, but don't overdo it. Unless you want to turn your lovable Corgi into an annoying pest, don't ever feed him from the table.

Although two males may not get along, for the most part, Corgis seem to do well with other pets in the household. Whether it's another Corgi or some other breed, if the dogs are introduced properly, you shouldn't have a problem. Corgis also seem to get along very well with cats. A friend of mine suggests it's because they are close to the same size, but most Corgis outweigh most cats. While individual Corgis may get along with individual guinea pigs, birds, hamsters, or even mice, remember that these same animals would be prey for a Corgi in the wild. Never leave any dog with any small pet unless you are closely supervising. Dog toys appeal to dogs because the toys make a high-pitched squeaky sound. Small, furry animals make a very similar sound. Keep those other pets safe, even if your Corgi seems inclined to be friendly.

Generally speaking, Corgis are friendly dogs, but as with any dog, socialization when the dog is young is an important part of his development. Any dog can be fearful, shy, or aggressive. It's up to you to introduce your Corgi to new people and places in a way that will make it all a positive experience and help your Corgi grow up to be a welcome addition to the family.

STANDARD for the Pembroke Welsh Corgi

The standard for the Pembroke Welsh Corgi is a clear, straightforward document that should help you to picture the ideal Corgi. Having a copy of the illustrated standard, published by the Pembroke Welsh Corgi Club of America, will help you understand each point with the help of pictures. The American Kennel Club's video of the Corgi standard is also a great way to study the breed, giving you the opportunity to see dogs in motion. Here, each section from the standard is followed by my brief remarks.

General Appearance. Low-set, strong, sturdily built and active, giving an impression of substance and stamina in a small space. Should not be so low and heavy-boned as to appear coarse or overdone, nor so light-boned as to appear racy. Outlook bold, but kindly. Expression intelligent and interested. Never shy nor vicious.

This pretty much says it all. Corgis are not toy dogs. They should be built to work, which means they should be solid, without being heavy and unable to move. They need to be able to dodge and turn after livestock. Their intelligent and interested expression makes them a joy to work with.

Corgis are not toy dogs. They should be built to work, which means they should be solid without being heavy and unable to move.

Corgis are longer than they are tall. The ideal male is between 27 and 30 pounds with bitches weighing slightly less.

Size and Proportions. Moderately long and low. The distance from the withers to base of tail should be approximately 40 percent greater than the distance from withers to ground. Height (from ground to highest point on withers) should be 10 to 12 inches. Weight is in proportion to size, not exceeding 30 pounds for dogs and 28 pounds for bitches. In show condition, the preferred medium-size dog of correct bone and substance will weigh approximately 27 pounds, with bitches approximately 25 pounds. Obvious oversized specimens and diminutive toy-like individuals must be very seriously penalized.

Again, a clear picture of Corgi size. Corgis are longer than they are tall, but not so long as a Dachshund. Anything over the weight limit mentioned would mean the dog is too heavy to be able to effectively work as a herding dog, losing flexibility with the gain in weight. A dog too small or too light would lack the endurance a Corgi needs in the field. While not too many Corgis work for a living today, that endurance and flexibility is an asset if you're competing in herding trials or agility.

Head and Skull. Head to be foxy in shape and appearance but not sly in expression. Skull should be fairly wide and flat between the ears. Moderate amount of stop. Very slight rounding of cheek, not filled in below the eyes, as foreface should be nicely chiseled to give a somewhat tapered muzzle. Distance from the occiput to center of stop to be greater than the distance from stop to nose tip, the proportion being five parts of total distance for the skull and three parts for the foreface. Muzzle should be neither dish-faced nor Roman-nosed. Nose is black and fully pigmented.

What they're measuring is from the back of the head to the stop, the place where the skull drops off to the muzzle. The Corgi's stop is well defined, not like a Borzoi or Collie stop. A domed head is not the look you want in a Corgi and neither is a short, snipy muzzle, nor a broad, heavy one. The image of a fox is a good example. A nice straight muzzle is next, slightly shorter than the head. You don't want a Collie muzzle, nor a blunt, short one. Young dogs may have some pink on their noses, but this should disappear with age. There should be no pink on an adult nose.

Eyes. Oval, medium in size, not round nor protruding, nor deepset and piglike. Set somewhat obliquely. Variations of brown in harmony with coat color. Eye rims dark, preferably black. While dark eyes enhance the expression, true black eyes are most undesirable, as are yellow or bluish eyes.

The Corgi should have a kindly, intelligent, alert expression.

The kindly, intelligent, alert look so desirable in a Corgi would be greatly distorted by deep-set or protruding eyes. Besides altering the look of a Corgi, these types of eyes would be susceptible to injury in the field. The dark eye rim draws attention to the expressive eyes.

Ears. Erect, firm, and of medium size, tapering slightly to a rounded point. Ears are mobile and react sensitively to sounds. A line drawn from the nose tip through the eyes to the ear tips and across should form an approximate equilateral triangle. Bat ears, small cat-like ears, overly large weak ears, hooded ears, or ears carried too high or too low are undesirable. Button, rose, or drop ears are very serious faults.

We're back to the foxy look again. The ears are a large factor in that look, and when placed properly on the head, contribute to the overall Corgi look.

Mouth. Scissors bite, the inner side of the upper incisors touching the outer side of the lower incisors. Level bite is acceptable. Lips should be black and tight, with little or no fullness. Overshot or undershot bite is a very serious fault.

Breed standards vary from country to country and from registry to registry. Become familiar with the standard that applies to your area.

The breed standard describes the ideal Pembroke Welsh Corgi. Most breeders keep this in mind when choosing their breeding stock.

While no herding dog should seriously bite the stock he is working, the Corgi may indeed nip the heels of the cattle or sheep. This becomes harder with an overshot or undershot jaw. Also, the versatility of a Corgi means that those jaws should be able to catch and kill mice and rats in the barn, earlier in the breed's history, those same jaws meant the Corgi could also retrieve game. A proper bite makes all of that possible.

Neck. Fairly long. Of sufficient length to provide over-all balance of the dog. Slightly arched, clean, and blending well into the shoulders. A very short neck giving a stuffy appearance and a long, thin, or ewe neck are faulty.

Balance is the key, not only in looks but also in movement. The neck described above helps balance the Corgi's length of body and helps give him flexibility.

Body. Rib cage should be well sprung, slightly egg-shaped, and moderately long. Deep chest, well let down between the forelegs. Exaggerated lowness interferes with the desired freedom of movement and should be penalized. Viewed from above, the body should taper slightly to end of loin. Loin short. Firm and level

The tail is docked as short as possible without being indented on the Corgi.

As a working dog, the Corgi needs to be able to move properly. The movement should be free and smooth.

topline, neither riding up to nor falling away at the croup. A slight depression behind the shoulders caused by heavier neck coat meeting the shorter body coat is permissible. Round or flat rib cage, lack of brisket, extreme length or cobbiness, are undesirable.

The well-sprung rib cage allows for plenty of room for the heart and lungs. A working dog needs to be able to fill his lungs to capacity. Too round or too flat a rib cage restricts the lungs and prevents them from working at their best.

Forequarters. Legs short; forearms turned slightly inward, with the instance between wrists less than between the shoulder joints, so that the front does not appear absolutely straight. Ample bone carried right down into the feet. Pasterns firm and nearly straight when viewed from the side. Weak pasterns and knuckling over are serious faults. Shoulder blades long and well laid back along the rib cage. Upper arms nearly equal in length to shoulder blades. Elbows parallel to the body, not prominent, and well set as to allow a line perpendicular to the ground to be drawn from the tip of the shoulder blade through to elbow.

The long, laid back shoulder blades mean the Corgi has a smooth, easy gait, with no wasted movement and no wasted energy. That's important in a working dog. Parallel elbows also contribute to a smooth, correct gait. A straight front would indicate a narrow rib cage, which in turn would mean not enough room for efficient breathing while working.

Hindquarters. Ample bone, strong and flexible, moderately angulated at stifle and hock. Exaggerated angulation is as faulty as too little. Thighs should be well muscled. Hocks short, parallel, and when viewed from the side are perpendicular to the ground. Barrel hocks or cowhocks are most objectionable. Slipped or double-jointed hocks are very faulty.

Well-muscled, moderately angulated rear legs give the Corgi the power and drive he needs when herding. The short hocks help with balance as the Corgi twists and turns in pursuit of cattle.

Tail. Docked as short as possible without being indented. Occasionally a puppy is born with a natural dock, which if sufficiently short is acceptable. A tail up to 2 inches in length is allowed, but if carried high tends to spoil the contour of the topline.

The theory is that the Corgi tail is docked to prevent a longer tail from becoming full of burrs or getting caught in brush. Although a tail of up to 2 inches in length is allowed in the standard, in practice, that much visible tail would indicate a pet Corgi and that dog and handler would have a hard time competing in conformation. In Britain, where only veterinarians may dock tails, many breeders are successfully breeding Corgis with natural bobtails.

Feet. Oval, with the two center toes slightly in advance of the two outer ones. Turning neither in nor out. Pads strong and feet arched. Nails short. Dewclaws on both forelegs and hind legs usually removed. Too round, long and narrow, or splayed feet are faulty.

Feet that turn in or out are not going to be as efficient in moving the Corgi forward at a good pace. Short nails prevent slipping, and there is less chance that a short nail will catch on something and tear. For this same reason, dewclaws are removed.

Movement. Free and smooth. Forelegs should reach well forward, without too much lift, in unison with the driving action of hind legs. The correct shoulder assembly and well-fitted elbows allow the

The coat should be of medium length with a short, thick, weather-resistant undercoat and a coarser, longer outer coat.

long, free stride in front. Viewed from the front, the legs do not move in exact parallel planes, but incline slightly inward to compensate for shortness of leg and width of chest. Hind legs should drive well under the body and move on a line with the forelegs with hocks turning neither in nor out. Feet must travel parallel to the line of motion, with no tendency to swing out, cross over, or interfere with each other. Short, choppy movement, rolling or high-stepping gait, close or overly wide coming or going, are incorrect. This is a herding dog that must have the agility, freedom of movement, and endurance to do the work for which he was developed.

That last sentence says it all. Herding dogs need to be able to move. The AKC video shows Corgi movement in slow motion, which can help you understand what this part of the standard describes.

Color. The outer coat is to be of self colors in red, sable, fawn, black and tan, with or without white markings. White is acceptable on legs, chest, neck (either in part or as a collar), muzzle, underparts, and as a narrow blaze on head.

Very Serious Faults (Color)

Whitelies: Body color white with red or dark markings.

Mismarks: Self colors with any area of white on the back between withers and tail, on sides between elbows and back of hindquarters, or on ears. Black and white markings with no tan present.

Bluies: Colored portions of the coat have a distinct bluish or smoky cast. This coloring is associated with extremely light or blue eyes and liver or gray eye rims, nose and lip pigment.

Color can range from a pale, sandy color up to a deep, rich red. Sable means that these red hairs are tipped with black. The black and tans generally have white as well and are referred to as tri-colors. Tri-colors also have their variations. They may be mostly black with tan over the eyes, on the cheeks, and at the tops of the legs, or they may be what is called a "redheaded tri" and have a tan head as well as the tan markings on the legs. The pattern may remind you of the coloring of a Beagle. Brindle coats and merles, both of which are permitted in Cardigan Welsh Corgis, are not permitted on a Pembroke Welsh Corgi.

Coat. Medium length; short, thick, weather-resistant undercoat with a coarser, longer outer coat. Over-all length varies, with slightly thicker and longer ruff around neck, chest, and on the shoulders. The body coat lies flat. Hair is slightly longer on back of forelegs and underparts and somewhat fuller and longer on rear of hindquarters. The coat is preferably straight, but some waviness is permitted. This breed has a shedding coat, and seasonal lack of undercoat should not be too severely penalized, providing the hair is glossy, healthy, and well groomed. A wiry, tightly marcelled coat is very faulty, as is an overly short, smooth, and thin coat. The Corgi should be shown in his natural condition, with no trimming permitted except to tidy the feet and, if desired, remove the whiskers.

Very Serious Fault (Coat)

Fluffies: A coat of extreme length with exaggerated feathering on ears, chest, legs and feet, underparts and hindquarters. Trimming such a coat does not make it any more acceptable.

Corgis definitely shed! If you don't like hair, you won't want a Corgi. The fluffies can look like a very small Collie. Some have so much hair, including undercoat, that they resemble small haystacks. Keeping up with a fluffy coat is a lot of work. The coat is also usually softer, which

A Corgi that closely matches the breed standard will make an impressive contender in the show ring.

means it will have more of a tendency to mat, as well as to collect and hold dirt.

Overall Picture. Correct type, including general balance and outline, attractiveness of headpiece, intelligent outlook, and correct temperament is of primary importance. Movement is especially important, particularly as viewed from the side. A dog with smooth and free gait has to be reasonably sound and must be highly regarded. A minor fault must never take precedence over the above desired qualities.

A dog must be very seriously penalized for the following faults, regardless of whatever desirable qualities the dog may present: whitelies, mismarks, or bluies; fluffies; button, rose, or drop ears; overshot or undershot bite; oversize or undersize.

The judge shall dismiss from the ring any Pembroke Welsh Corgi that is vicious or excessively shy.

Note that there are several serious faults, but only those relating to temperament are cause for ring dismissal. A Corgi must have the correct temperament. The other faults, while detracting from the ideal, don't affect temperament. If you have a fluffy or a mismark as a pet, you can't show the dog in conformation, but you may compete in performance events, and you will still have a terrific pet.

SELECTING Your Corgi

There is no one hard and fast rule for choosing the Corgi puppy that will be right for you and your family. My best advice is to listen to the breeder. He or she will know his or her own line and what the puppies are likely to be like as adults. He or she wants the best possible match between puppy and new owner. Just as not every breed is right for every person, not every Corgi is right for every person. Be honest with your breeder so that everyone is happy.

WHERE TO FIND YOUR PUPPY

Because your Corgi will be a member of the family for 12 to 14 years, take the time to make the right match.

Breeders

Start with finding a breeder you can work with. The Pembroke Welsh Corgi Club of America has a list of its members online. While there's no guarantee that all the breeders on the list are

If buying your Corgi from a breeder, make sure that her pups are kept in a clean environment.

reputable, the odds are good that they will be. Being a member of the national club means these people have committed a large amount of time and energy to the breed. In the case of the Pembroke Welsh Corgi Club, applicants for membership must have been involved with the breed for at least five years and must have two sponsors who have known them for at least two years. The American Kennel Club website also has links to breeders. Again, there's no guarantee that every breeder is reputable, but it's a good place to start.

Talk to several breeders. A person may be a wonderful breeder, but if you're not comfortable talking with him or her, find someone else. You want to be able to contact this breeder when you have questions about your Corgi. The most valuable thing a breeder can give you, besides the puppy, is his or her phone number.

Dog Shows

Another place to find a breeder is at a dog show. All exhibitors are listed in the back of the catalog, and the list includes their addresses. Talk to the Corgi people at a show and ask questions about temperament, grooming, and exercise. Watch the Corgis in the ring. If one catches your eye, maybe you can get a related puppy. Just remember, while you may be able to exchange a word or two ringside before the dog is shown at a dog show, save the long conversations for after the handler and dog have been in the ring. Handlers may be trying to watch the judge so they'll be aware of the pattern the judge is using to gait each dog. They may be trying to settle their dog or get him excited. They are concentrating on their dog and may be abrupt if you start asking questions. Talk to them after they've shown, and the odds are good they'll be more than happy to help.

Rescue Organizations

Rescue organizations are another source to explore. Just because a dog is in rescue doesn't mean there is anything wrong with him. It may be that someone hasn't done the homework necessary for selecting a particular breed of dog. They may have gotten a Corgi puppy and found he needed more exercise than they could give, or there was more hair than they expected. A divorce may mean the family dog is surrendered to rescue. Someone in the family may be allergic to dogs. You might avoid the puppy stage altogether and be

If you decide to get your dog from a rescue organization, inspect the facilities and make sure that the dogs are well cared for.

able to adopt a dog that is already partly trained. The dog will also be spayed or neutered, as it is very rare for a rescue organization to let any dog go to a new home without the dog being spayed or neutered.

A rescue organization will ask as many questions as a breeder because it wants to find a permanent home for its charges. Don't take offense at these questions. Rescue organizations want the best match possible between dog and family, and they want the placement to last. A rescue dog may already have been in two or three homes, so the rescuers will be determined to find him a permanent home.

Animal Shelters

Another possible source may be your local animal shelter. Corgis are not commonly found in shelters, but it can happen. Many shelters will keep a list of potential adopters, along with their breed preference. If they don't offer such a service, make it a habit to call the shelter once a month or so. You might also want to stop by in person to see the available dogs. Not every shelter employee will know every breed of dog, and Corgis still aren't that common.

As cute as puppies are, there can be advantages to getting an adult. For one thing, an adult will probably, although not always, be housetrained. As an adult, they can also wait longer before having to go out. This means you can skip the housetraining stage and may not have to worry as much about accidents in the house. Another advantage to an adult is that he will probably already know some basic commands. He will have outgrown the puppy urge to chew everything in sight.

Conversely, an adult may come with habits or problems that you will have to learn about and deal with. The habit could be something minor, like jumping on the couch, or it could be something more serious, like a dog that is food aggressive or afraid of children. While most rescue organizations have the dogs in foster care to determine just what, if any, problems there might be, animal shelters don't usually have the staff or the time to be able to tell what problems exist. You may trade housetraining time for retraining time.

No matter what source you try, don't expect to get a dog immediately. If you're trying to get a puppy from a breeder, understand that responsible breeders are probably not going to have more than a couple of litters a year. When you call, they may not

If you don't have the time to properly take care of a Corgi pup, you may decide that adopting an adult dog is right for you. Just remember that an adult dog may also have his training problems.

be planning to have any puppies for six months or more. Also, breeders frequently have waiting lists for their puppies. Even being on a list doesn't guarantee you a puppy. If there are five people waiting and there are only two puppies, three families are going to be disappointed.

FINDING THE RIGHT DOG

First, don't be too firm about what you want. Don't demand a red and white female or nothing at all. What if all the girls in the litter are tri-colored or sable? What if there are no girls? There's not much difference between male and female Corgis. They are very close in size, and both sexes are intelligent and loving. My males have been a bit more protective than the females and a bit more apt to bark, but not excessively so. A female may be a bit more inclined to cuddle, but I've know very cuddly males, too.

A male will housetrain as easily as a female but, especially if exposed to intact females, may lift his leg against furniture as a way to mark his territory. Neutering at an early age usually (but not always) prevents this. If the dog is a show prospect, you may not neuter while showing, and this means you will have to be

39

ready to deal with this behavior if it starts. With females, unless spayed, you must deal with twice yearly heat cycles. If you are not planning to show, both sexes should be neutered. This will not affect their personalities and will make them much easier to live with as pets.

A good breeder is going to try to make the best match between you and the puppy. It may be that for your lifestyle, the tri-color male is a better match than the red and white female. A trainer I know once spoke of a particular dog, saying, "Would he be my choice for a family that had never had a dog before? No. Would he be my choice for obedience competition? Absolutely."

Listen to your breeder and be flexible. I guarantee that a male Corgi is going to worm his way into your heart just as quickly as the female Corgi. Having said that, don't let yourself be talked into a puppy you just don't want. No matter what the outcome of the temperament test or the breeder's assessment of which puppy would be best for your household, if you know you will never be able to deal calmly with a leg-lifting male, hold out for a female. It

Don't take the first puppy you see. Play with the pups for a while to see which one will make the best pet.

may mean a longer wait or going to another breeder, but when you choose a puppy, it should be for life.

You might want to consider an older dog instead of a puppy. While puppies are a delight and loads of fun, maybe an older dog would be even better. Perhaps a breeder has a young dog he or she's kept because he or she wanted to see if he'd be a good show dog. Maybe he didn't mature as the breeder had hoped he would. This could be your perfect pet. In all likelihood, he will be housetrained and he may even know a few basic commands. You'll still have a breeder to depend on when you have questions, but you'll also have an older dog that may be past the teething stage and will be able to be left alone for longer periods of time.

HEALTH CONCERNS

Whether you decide on a puppy or an adult, there are things to look for and questions to ask to help ensure you are getting a healthy dog. For starters, look at the puppies' eyes and noses. Both should be clear, with no discharge. The puppies should be alert and lively. It's all right to feel sorry for the droopy little pup in the corner, but he's probably not the one you should take home. Most breeders give you 48 to 72 hours to have your choice checked by a veterinarian before the sale is final, and there are lemon laws in many states to assure that you have a healthy dog, but why start out asking for trouble? Take home a healthy pup to begin with. You should also be taking home the health records for that puppy, which should tell you the dates the puppy was wormed and what shots have been given. Also, be sure to meet one or both of the parent dogs. It's likely that the puppies will take after their parents in size and temperament. A shy, fearful parent is not a good beginning.

Von Willebrand's Disease

Responsible Corgi breeders test their stock and are careful not to breed animals with known problems. Corgis are a fairly healthy breed, but one of the diseases they may carry is von Willebrand's, a blood disorder. With von Willebrand's, as opposed to hemophilia, the dog doesn't start bleeding right away, but uses up his limited amount of clotting factor. If surgery is necessary and it is known ahead of time that a dog has the disease, plasma can be supplied. Ask your breeder if he or she has tested the parents for von Willebrand's, and if so, what the result was.

Corgis and children usually make great friends. Always supervise all interactions to make sure that both child and dog are safe.

Progressive Retinal Atrophy (PRA)

Progressive Retinal Atrophy (PRA) in Corgis seems to be an inherited disease, and so breeders should be vigilant about eye testing. The parents should be tested, as should the puppies.

Hip Displasia

Hip displasia can occur in any breed, but it is not much of a problem in Corgis. I would not reject a puppy just because his parents weren't tested, but many Corgi breeders do x-ray their dogs' hips and obtain a rating from the Orthopedic Foundation for Animals (OFA) or from the University of Pennsylvania Hip Improvement Program (PennHip). If this is a concern of yours, choose your puppy from stock that has had its hips tested.

PET-QUALITY OR SHOW-QUALITY PUPPY?

Do you want a pet-quality or a show-quality puppy? These two terms will likely be in the contract you and the breeder sign. Neither term should have anything to do with health or temperament. Your puppy should be in good health and have the proper Corgi temperament, whether you want a pet or whether you want to show your dog. Calling a dog show quality is not a guarantee that the dog will ever become a champion. Show quality means that the dog meets the standard and has no serious faults that would hinder him from winning. A show-quality Corgi will have a proper bite, will not be a fluffy, will have proper coloration, and will otherwise conform to the standard.

A pet-quality Corgi may be a fluffy or may be mismarked. The teeth may be undershot or overshot. If the dog is a male, he may have an undescended testicle. All of these things would make it hard, if not impossible, to win in the conformation ring, but none of them would stop the dog from being a loving family companion or from being able to compete in many of the performance events. A breeder may also classify a puppy as pet quality even if he meets the standard physically, if he doesn't have the personality for the conformation ring. Successful show dogs need to look alert and lively in the ring. A dog that hates to show, that lags at the end of the lead, and has ears that stick straight out, or are always back, is not going to win, no matter how gorgeous he is physically.

The price for a pet-quality puppy is usually less than the price for a show-quality puppy. Also, the contract will call for the pet puppy to be spayed or neutered. The breeder may give you a limited registration. The AKC offers limited registration, which means that the offspring of a particular dog may not be registered with the AKC. This helps ensure that a buyer will not breed what a breeder considers a pet-quality dog. The limited registration may be changed to a full registration if, as the dog matures, the breeder feels the quality has changed.

No matter what kind of registration the breeder offers, those registration papers should be given to you when you get your puppy. In the United States, the dog will most likely be registered with the AKC, but he might be registered with the United Kennel Club. If your puppy is from Canada, the papers should be from the Canadian Kennel Club.

You should also receive a copy of your puppy's pedigree when you receive the registration papers. This is a family tree indicating your puppy's ancestors, and it should go back at least three generations.

Depending on how old the puppy is when you get him, several vaccinations may have been given. The age at which a puppy should go to a new home is a frequently argued question. Some say that at 7 weeks old a puppy is ready to bond to humans and to leave his littermates and dam. However, many breeders refuse to let a puppy go before eight weeks. Others believe that eight weeks is an age when puppies may be fearful of new events, and that it is better to wait until the puppy is nine weeks old. Many breeders prefer to keep their puppies until they are twelve weeks old, starting the crate training and housetraining themselves and making sure that the puppies have all of the necessary vaccinations before they go to their new homes.

Many people think that if they don't get their puppy as young as possible, the dog won't bond with them. This is not true. Puppies are very adaptable and will quickly adopt and love new humans as quickly as the new humans adopt and love them! Even most adult dogs will transfer their love and loyalty to their new family, as well, so if you're considering an older rescue dog, don't hesitate because you're afraid you won't bond.

QUESTIONS FROM THE BREEDER

Just as you will have questions for the breeder, the breeder will have questions for you. Don't be offended. The breeder has put a

When visiting a breeder, her Pembroke Welsh Corgis should look healthy and loved. They should not shy away from people

lot of time and effort and money into producing the litter of puppies, and he or she wants to make sure they go to a good home and will be properly taken car of.

Kathy Smith of Cymry Corgis in Vermont sends prospective puppy buyers a questionnaire. Any responsible breeder will ask many of these same questions, although they may not be in written form. Here's the Cymry questionnaire.

As each puppy is an individual, this questionnaire will help us determine which puppy might best fit your lifestyle.

1. How did you hear about us?

2. The Welsh Corgi, Pembroke is also not extremely well known. How did you become interested in the breed? Have you ever seen

Before you select a Pembroke Welsh Corgi, you need to decide whether you want a pet- or show-quality dog.

a Pem? Do you know someone who owns one?

3. If you own or have owned a Corgi in the past, please let us know from whom you obtained your dog. If it was some time ago that you had the dog, when was it?

4. The Welsh Corgi is a herding dog. This is a breed used for driving cattle, sheep, geese, etc. Will this pose a problem in your household or lifestyle?

5. Have you read any books about the breed? If so, which ones?

6. What are your expectations for your dog? Pet, show, companion...what words would you use to describe what you would like in a dog?

7. Do you have a preference for a male or a female puppy? Would you take a puppy of the opposite sex should your first choice not be available? If not, what creates the preference?

8. Would you be interested in an older puppy or an adult?

9. Tell us a bit about your household. Spouse, partner, or roommates? Children and their ages?

10. Do any family members suffer from allergies?

11. Who will be responsible for the care and training of your pet?

12. Would you call your family more the "outdoors-type " or "homebodies?"

13. In what family activities would you include your dog?

14. Have you ever had a dog before? Do you have any pets at this time (other dogs, cats, birds, fish, etc.)?

15. Please tell us a little bit about your previous pet owning experiences (use extra paper if necessary):

16. Do you have a veterinarian your family uses or has used in the past? If yes, please provide the name, address, and telephone number.

17. Do you live in a house, townhouse, Condo, apartment? If so, how large is your yard and what type of fencing do you have? Please describe, including height.

18. If you rent, does your landlord/landlady allow you to have a dog? Please provide the landlord/landlady's contact information.

19. Corgis are athletic dogs that require regular exercise. This could mean daily walks on lead, swimming, hiking, running, games of fetch, or playing with other dogs in a secure area. Have you thought about how you will handle your dog's exercise needs? Please describe.

20. In what rooms inside your home will your dog be permitted?

Do you have any ideas about how you will keep your dog out of certain parts of your home, if necessary?

21. Have you thought about housetraining a puppy and handling an adult dog? What about "bathroom" needs? Where will your dog go to eliminate? How will you clean up?

22. How many hours each day will your dog be left alone while you're at work? Do you have a secure place to leave your pet while you are away from home? Where will your pet sleep at night?

23. If travel plans took you away from home, what arrangements would you make for your dog? Boarding kennel? Pet sitter? Neighbors or relatives? Take your dog with you?

24. Training and proper socialization are important to a puppy's development into a secure and happy adult companion. Can you devote the time needed during the critical first few months to teach manners and expose your puppy to many new experiences? Do you have any ideas about where you would go for obedience training or socialization? Additional comments or thoughts.

It's a long list but you can see that responsible breeders want the best for their puppies, and, they want to make sure that you understand exactly what is involved in owning a Corgi. Answering these questions ahead of time will help you to think about your puppy's needs and just how you will meet them. With luck, that puppy will be a loving companion for many years.

CARING for Your Corgi

You've made your selection, and your Corgi puppy is joining your family for many years of love and companionship. Your puppy should not have any evidence of fleas or ticks and should have been wormed, since most puppies are born with roundworms. These are typically tested for and treated at ages two, four, six, and eight weeks. Your breeder should supply the dates and the kind of medicine used.

Depending on the age of your puppy, he may or may not have received his first set of vaccinations. Currently, many veterinarians give the first set of shots at 8 weeks, then 12 weeks, 16 weeks, and then annually after that, although some veterinarians may also recommend shots at 18 to 20 weeks, and then annually. Check with the breeder to see what, if any, shots have been given to your puppy. Usually, the shots given are combination vaccinations that include protection against distemper, leptospirosis, hepatitis, parvovirus, and may or may not also include parainfluenza.

An inoculation against rabies is required in every state, but the time span between shots may differ. Some states require a rabies shot every year, some every three years. Check with your veterinarian for your state's requirements.

CHOOSING A VETERINARIAN

No matter how old your puppy is, or what shots he has received, the first thing you should do is make an appointment to have him looked at by

A happy, health pup only stays happy and healthy if properly cared for. Make sure that you take your dog regularly to visit his veterinarian.

your veterinarian. If you don't have a veterinarian, try to find one before the puppy comes home. Depending on your contract with the breeder, there will be a specified window of time for getting a clean bill of health. The time limit may be anywhere from 48 hours to one month, with the shorter time frame more common. If your puppy hasn't received all of his shots, this initial visit becomes even more important. Both distemper and parvovirus are often fatal in puppies, so this is not a visit to ignore or postpone.

Ask friends who have pets which veterinarian they go to and why they chose him or her. If they have a complaint about a particular practice, is it legitimate? Think about whether you want to take your dog to a large practice, with multiple doctors, or to a smaller practice. There can be advantages to both. In a small practice, the veterinarian may get to know you and your dog better than if you see different doctors on different visits. The disadvantage is that if your veterinarian is on vacation or ill, a veterinarian from a different practice won't know you at all. In an emergency, that vet won't have any background on your pet. With a larger practice, while a particular veterinarian might not really know you, he or she will have your pet's entire medical history easily accessible.

Distance may determine which veterinarian you go to. If you've obtained recommendations for more than one practice, you may want the one closest to your home. Or, maybe there's a practice where one of the veterinarians has Corgis, which may appeal to you.

Consider the practice's response to emergencies. Is there someone on call at night and on holidays? Does the staff seem willing to squeeze you in if there's a sudden problem, or do they brush you off? Are the offices and waiting room clean? Will the veterinarian take the time to explain what he or she is doing?

You may not be able to answer all these questions without a visit or two to the office, but if anything makes you uncomfortable, find another veterinarian. Even if everything about the office is perfect, if you aren't happy with the veterinarian for whatever reason, go elsewhere. You want someone who can care for your pet, of course, but you also want someone you are comfortable around, who will talk to you about your pet's care, and who will answer your questions. You also want someone who will listen to you. Even the best veterinarian won't know your dog as well as you will. Ideally, you and your veterinarian will be partners, working to keep your dog healthy.

If your Corgi should have an accident or become ill, you need to take him to see the vet to get the proper treatment.

Corgi puppies are so cute that the veterinary staff will probably pay some extra attention to your puppy before the examination. This will be good for the puppy, as it will give him a pleasant association with the office, not just the unpleasant memory of a shot.

At this first appointment, if you have any concerns at all or any questions about proper health care, ask your vet. If you are uncomfortable about brushing your puppy's teeth, for example, ask for a demonstration and discuss different methods. Ask about flea and tick protection and about heartworm prevention. Ask if there are any specific health concerns related to your part of the country, such as Lyme disease. Your dog's health will be your responsibility for the next 12 to 14 years, so start off right.

FEEDING YOUR PUPPY

The next major concern is food. By the time you get your puppy, the breeder will have weaned him from his mother, gradually introducing solid foods until he is eating a quality puppy food. Your

The number of feedings and the amount fed will vary as your Pembroke Welsh Corgi gets older. Ask your veterinarian or breeder for help in setting up a feeding schedule.

breeder should give you a three or four-day supply of whatever food the puppy is used to, but it is up to you to decide if you will continue with this brand or switch to another. If you decide to switch, remember to do so gradually, over a period of about a week, so that the puppy's system can also make the change without an upset stomach or diarrhea.

With larger breeds, the advice now is to switch to an adult food as soon as possible. Many veterinarians recommend this with Corgis as well, so that when the dog is about six months old, he is introduced to an adult food.

Choosing a Brand

There are dozens of brands of dog food on the market, and while many are high quality, not all are right for every dog. Even within a breed, one brand may be too rich for an individual dog, or not be well tolerated by a dog. Right now, I have three Corgis, and all three are on a different kind of food. Griffin is allergic to corn and lamb, so he's on a chicken and rice dry-food diet. Rhiannon is on a premium lamb and rice food because her breeder recommended it and she is doing well with it. Her coat is shiny and her stools are small, indicating that she is using most of what she eats. Hayley is on a veterinarian-recommended canned food diet because she's been diagnosed with lymphoma.

Ask your breeder what adult food his or her dogs eat. Ask friends. Observe your dog and see how he responds to the food. Does he eat it quickly and seem to enjoy it? Check his stools; are they firm? Is his coat in good condition, or is it dull or brittle? A Corgi's coat should have the luster of good health.

Types
You'll also have to decide on dry, semi-moist, or canned food. Dry food is generally cheaper and provides your dog with something to chew, although many Corgis seem to bolt their food, with no thought of chewing. Semi-moist foods tend to have more sugar in them than is necessary, as well as more dyes and preservatives. Canned foods definitely appeal to dogs. These foods smell good, at least to dogs, and may have more meat in them. They also contain water and will cost more than the dry foods.

Ingredients
When choosing a food, check the list of ingredients. Two of the first five ingredients should be an animal-based protein, and ideally,

Many vets recommend hard kibble as part of a dog's nutritional needs. Not only is it healthy for your dog, but the texture can also help in keeping your dog's teeth clean.

If you give your Pembroke Welsh Corgi treats throughout the day, remember that these treats should be nutritious and are a part of his daily food intake.

one of those should be in the first position. Chicken, beef, and lamb are the usual kinds of meat you'll find listed. Premium dog foods offer a balanced diet for your dog, with necessary vitamins and minerals. If you feed a balanced food, you shouldn't need supplements. Commercially prepared foods are the easiest, cheapest way to feed your Corgi. Whatever kind of food you choose, dry or canned, it all should meet the standards set by AAFCO, the Association of American Food Control Officials. Meeting these standards guarantees certain levels of ingredients and assures that the basic nutritional needs of your dog are being met. More detailed information on AAFCO may be found at their website.

All-Natural Diets and Cooking for Your Dog

All-natural diets are gaining in popularity, as are home-cooked meals. If you decide to prepare your Corgi's food yourself, be aware that he still needs a balanced diet. Cooking up some ground meat or chicken and adding some boiled rice may be fine to help correct the occasional upset stomach, but it is not a balanced diet. Bones with the meat attached are not balanced. There is also some concern about bacteria in raw meat and eggs and about problems caused by bones. Some veterinarians are totally against feeding raw meat because of the health threat; others say that the benefits outweigh the possible danger.

Seriously cooking for your dog means adding vegetables as well as vitamins and minerals. Your Corgi will need a balanced diet. There are some excellent books on the subject of natural feeding versus commercial foods. If this is what you prefer, and you have the time to spend, research the subject thoroughly. Two good web sites are www.stevesrealfood.com and www.petdiets.com. You'll find information on the thinking behind feeding raw foods, as well as answers to questions you may have. At www.petdiets.com, they will even help you formulate a diet just for your dog. Try to talk to an animal nutritionist if you are serious about cooking for your dog.

Keep in mind that if you decide to prepare your dog's food yourself, a significant amount of time and dedication will be required, and there will be no vacations from that work. Make sure you have freezer or refrigerator room for the food as well.

Whatever food you choose, feed your dog from a clean dish, and make sure he always has access to fresh, clean water. The kind of dish doesn't make much difference. Stainless steel is easy to clean and is nonbreakable. If you decide on that adorable ceramic bowl decorated with bones, make sure the paint and glaze are lead-free. Hard plastic is another choice, although it may be harder to keep clean. No matter what kind of dish you use, do make sure you wash it after every meal. Just because your dog has licked the bowl clean doesn't mean it is clean. You wouldn't use your dinner dishes over and over without washing them.

Where to Feed

If you have more than one dog, feed them in separate areas so that there's no argument over the food. You don't want the dominant dog to get all the food, and you certainly don't want a dogfight. Feeding dogs in separate areas or in crates also makes sure that each dog gets whatever may be added to his food, like a supplement or a medicine. When dogs are fed separately, you can tell if one is off his food or hasn't eaten his heartworm pill.

BEDDING: INVESTING IN A CRATE

The next thing to think about is where your puppy is going to sleep. A crate is one of the best investments you can make. A good crate will outlast your dog and will pay for itself with its usefulness. Dogs are den animals, and a dog does not look at a crate as a cage or a jail. To a dog, it's a cozy, safe space that belongs to him. A crate offers a place where you can put your puppy to keep him safe when you can't watch him, or when you go out. A crate helps make housetraining easier as well, because no dog wants to relieve himself where he sleeps. If the puppy does have an accident in the crate, it's in a small, contained area that is easy to clean. Many wire crates have removable trays, which makes cleanup even easier. If you do choose a wire crate, drape a blanket or towels over it to enclose it and increase the den-like feel.

If you live in a small apartment or just don't have enough room for a large crate, you may want to get one that folds down so it can be stored away when not in use. The Nylabone® Fold-Away Pet Carrier sets up easily and folds down quickly. When not in use it can be stored behind a door or under your bed. Because it is easy to fold down and set up, it is ideal when traveling.

While you may be tempted by one of the many plush beds with attractive outer covers, wait until your dog is an adult before you invest. Puppies tend to chew on their bedding and, if they've had an accident, those foam-filled dog beds are harder to wash and take much longer to dry than a few old bath towels. Old towels or a flannel sheet, or pieces of fake fleece all provide a warm, soft bed that's easy to clean, and it won't matter if the puppy chews a hole in one of them.

Locate the crate wherever the family is most likely to gather. A kitchen is a good choice because of the activity and because there's usually a door from the kitchen to the outside, which makes it convenient for taking the puppy out. If possible, move the crate to a bedroom at night, or get a second crate for the bedroom. Corgi puppies like to be with their family. Letting the puppy sleep in a bedroom gives them eight hours of contact, and you don't even have to do anything. Another advantage to having the puppy in a bedroom is that if he wakes up in the middle of the night and has to "go," you'll hear him and be able to take him out.

Just remember that a crate is a wonderful tool, but it's not meant to be your puppy's permanent residence. Your puppy needs to have

A crate is an essential training tool. The Nylabone® Fold-Away Pet Carrier makes crate training easier and helps with housetraining.

playtime, both in the house and outdoors. Although there may be the occasional exception, don't crate your puppy for more than four hours at a time.

TOYS

Besides supplying food and a place to sleep, your puppy will need some toys to keep him active and stimulate his brain. Puppies seem to enjoy stuffed toys. Maybe it reminds them of their littermates, but you will frequently see a puppy sleeping curled up next to a favorite plush toy. Stuffed toys for dogs usually have a squeaker or two buried inside, and as the puppy grows, he will probably try to "kill" the toy by biting and digging to get at the squeaker. Watch the way your puppy plays. If he is tearing a hole in the toy, it's time to take it away. At this point, you can either throw the toy away or remove the stuffing and the squeaker and give the "skin" back to the puppy. Most stuffed toys are stuffed with some kind of synthetic cotton, which is not good for dogs to swallow. Once it's removed, your puppy may still enjoy dragging around the outer fabric. Keep an eye on him, though. If he settles down for a serious chew, he could swallow large pieces of the toy and either choke or end up with an intestinal obstruction.

Your Corgi puppy will also enjoy latex squeaky toys. Again, supervise. Many dogs will go right for the squeaky part. I frequently cut this part out, leaving just the latex. If your puppy accidentally swallows small pieces of latex, they should just pass through him harmlessly. One of my puppies once bit off every quill on a latex hedgehog with no ill effects (except to the hedgehog).

Puppies love to chew, especially when they're teething, so it's a good idea to always have something besides chair legs for them to gnaw on. Nylon bones and pressed rawhide bones are a good choice. Real bones are too apt to splinter, or as the dog gets older, he might actually bite off and swallow pieces that could lead to an impacted bowel. Many dogs manage to eat rawhide with no ill effects, but many others end up biting off and swallowing large chunks that can all end up in an indigestible lump in the stomach. Bones made of pressed rawhide are tiny pieces of rawhide heated and shaped. There's no large mass to cause a problem.

Cow hooves have been popular for a while now, but I find them too smelly for indoor use, and again, sharp pieces may cause a problem for your Corgi. I prefer the nylon bones because they are odorless to humans and don't stain carpeting or upholstery as some rawhide may do.

For outdoor fun, most Corgis love chasing plastic discs, and indoors or out, an old tennis ball will be retrieved for as long as you can throw it. If you're going to use a flying disc, keep it low. Leaping and twisting may cause back injuries in your Corgi.

EXERCISE

Your Corgi will need playtime and exercise all his life. As a small puppy, playtime should be short, with lots of time for naps in between play sessions. As your Corgi grows, you can both enjoy games like hide-and-seek and retrieving. A brisk walk around the neighborhood will stimulate both your Corgi's body and his mind, and as he matures, you may find that he likes a good game of football or soccer. Obedience classes or agility are also good outlets for the seemingly endless amount of energy your Corgi has.

A variety of chew toys, such as those made by Nylabone®, will help to keep your Pembroke Welsh Corgi busy when you can't keep an eye on him. They also make great rewards when training him.

Collars

For those long walks and obedience lessons, invest in a good collar and lead. No matter what kind of a collar you choose, make sure you check the size as your puppy grows. The collar that fits a three-month-old is not going to work on a six-month-old. Until your puppy is full grown, you might want to use a flat nylon buckle collar that lets you just push the tongue of the buckle through the fabric of the collar, giving you some flexibility in the size and saving the cost of a new collar. The time to invest in a good leather collar is when your dog is fully grown.

If you've decided to use a training collar for walks and classes, remember that these collars should never be left on your dog when he is unattended. It's all too easy for the ring on a training collar to get caught on something, and your dog could choke to death. Never, ever tie out a dog on a training collar for the same reason.

Head halters can work well, especially if you have a dog that insists on pulling. Most dogs seem to adjust quickly to these, although they will frequently put up a fight in the beginning. When you've first fitted your Corgi for a head halter, keep his head up. If he can get his head down, he will use his paws to scrape off the halter; once he knows it can be done, getting him to accept it will be that much harder. It won't take long before he is walking nicely and totally ignoring the halter.

While a harness is a must for tracking, it is not recommended for everyday walks. A harness doesn't give you much control over your dog, and it gives your dog more opportunity to pull.

Whatever kind of collar you choose, make sure you have a good lead. I prefer leather because it feels good, lasts a long time, and has a flexibility I like. Nylon web is also fine. Avoid chain leads with a little loop at the top. If you need to grab more of the lead for any reason, the chain will not be comfortable, and if your Corgi makes a dash while you're holding the chain, it can rip some skin off your hands.

Outside of a balanced diet, exercise, and vaccinations, your Corgi shouldn't need much in the way of special treatment. However, you will want to be careful about how much jumping your Corgi does off of high surfaces. Corgis are fearless and think nothing of jumping on and off of furniture. The height of a grooming table won't stop them from jumping, but you should. A Corgi's back is not as long proportionately as a Dachshund's, but

Exercise is important for any dog. The Corgi loves to be taken outside for some fun.

because they have such short legs, they can easily harm themselves jumping. Help your Corgi down from the couch or your bed and, if you have a van or a truck, help him out, rather than just letting him jump to the ground.

GROOMING

Your Corgi will need some grooming, but it's nothing you can't do right at home. There's no need for regularly scheduled sessions at your local groomer's. I recommend a grooming table, or some other way to get the Corgi up to your level. It's no fun trying to remove your dog's winter coat while you're on your hands and knees. If you don't want to buy a special grooming table, find another surface that will work. That could be a sturdy old table in your basement or garage. Cover it with a piece of rubber matting so your dog won't slip, and you're ready to go. For a while, I used the top of my clothes dryer with a rubber mat on it.

Besides getting your Corgi up to a comfortable level for you, it will help keep him in one spot. An advantage to an actual grooming

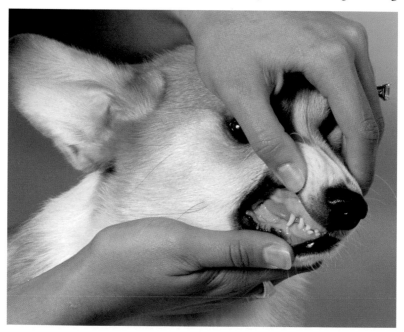

Your Pembroke Welsh Corgi needs to have his teeth checked regularly. If you notice plaque buildup, contact your veterinarian to have them cleaned.

table is that they come with a grooming arm, a post to which you can attach a grooming loop, which keeps your dog's head up and out of the way. That can be very helpful when you're trimming your Corgi's nails. Corgis are notorious for not wanting anyone to handle their feet.

Nail Care

Since we're on the subject of feet, let's start there for grooming. Unless you are taking long, regular walks on rough surfaces like a concrete sidewalk, your dog's nails will need to be cut. Long nails make walking harder for your Corgi and will eventually lead to splayed feet. Start handling his feet when your Corgi is young, and get him used to the clippers. To start with, just trim one or two nails, give him a treat, and let him go.

Many of my Corgis have accepted grinding more willingly than nail clippers. You can find grinders at many pet supply stores, in catalogs, and online. The grinder is an electric or battery-operated tool that has an abrasive wheel that grinds the nail, rather than cutting it. If you decide on a grinder, get your dog used to it gradually.

Start by putting the grinder on the grooming table and letting your dog smell it. Give him treats. Turn the machine on and give him some more treats. Next, put his foot on the handle of the grinder while it's running, letting him get used to the vibration. As with the nail clippers, you might want to just grind one or two nails, or those on just one foot before treating and releasing.

Your dog may still struggle in the beginning. When I first started grinding Rhiannon's nails, I had to hang on tight because she did struggle. Gentle but firm is the approach here. Now she stands quietly and lets me grind away. I am still careful to restrain her head when I do her front feet, as she would like to put her nose down to see what's going on, and a whirling grinding wheel and a dog's sensitive nose is not a good combination.

Once you've got your dog's nails done, lift each foot and trim the fur around the pads. This will help your dog's traction, especially in the winter when there's ice underfoot. A word of caution: If your dog is just wiggling too much and you can't be sure of cutting the fur without cutting the foot, stop. Either have a groomer take care of the foot fur, or let it grow. It's better to have it removed, but it's even better not to cut your dog. This holds true for nails, too. If you

All dogs need to have their nails trimmed from time to time. Use a clipper or a grinder to trim the nail to an appropriate length.

just can't get those nails shortened, have your veterinarian or a groomer do it for you. Nails need to be cut, so if you can't do it successfully, get someone who can.

Coat Care

To take care of your Corgi's coat, you'll need a good dog comb and a slicker brush. You may also want to buy some kind of a shedding rake for the times when your Corgi is loosing all of his undercoat at once. Corgis shed all year round, but twice a year they shed heavily in preparation for an all-new undercoat. These heavy sheds are usually in the spring and fall. There is also a brush similar to a currycomb for horses that is very good at loosening and removing dead guard hairs.

Before you begin grooming, spray the coat with a fine mist of water. You want the coat slightly damp, not soaking wet. I add a very small amount of mouthwash to the water. It smells good and helps a bit as a cleaning agent.

Start at your Corgi's rump and use your hand to push the coat the wrong way. Using the slicker brush, work at the bottom of the

Pembroke Welsh Corgis should be thoroughly brushed at least twice weekly. Always brush the coat in the direction that it naturally lies.

hair you've pushed back, using short, quick strokes to put it back in place, removing loose undercoat as you do so. This is harder to explain than it is to do, so you may want to ask your breeder or a groomer to show you.

Work through your dog's entire coat. Then use your comb to get even more of the coat. With the comb, you can work in the direction the hair is growing. Don't forget your Corgi's "pants," the longer hair on the hind legs. A comb works well on this, but again, work from the base of the hair. This will prevent pulling.

Bathing

Clean the inside of the ear with a damp cotton ball, being careful not to push into the ear canal. Wipe the corners of the eyes with a damp cloth or cotton ball as well.

That's all your Corgi needs. If you're grooming for the show ring, you may want to wash his feet with a waterless shampoo or work in some cornstarch, talcum powder, or chalk, but otherwise, grooming a Corgi is simple. There's no clipping or trimming required, besides foot fur. If you're showing your dog, you'll want to groom him every other day at least, but if he's a pet, once a week will keep him looking and feeling great.

Unless you're planning to show your dog, he won't need very many baths, especially if you brush him on a regular basis. A bath can help loosen the undercoat when your dog is heavily shedding in the spring and fall. Before any bath, brush thoroughly to get as much dead hair out before the bath as is possible. Brush after the bath to remove the hairs that the water and soap have loosened.

Some Corgis will fit in a laundry sink, which will again help your back. Otherwise, a regular tub will work. Use warm water and wet your dog thoroughly. Work in some dog shampoo. Don't use shampoos made for people, as the pH will not be the same and may dry your dog's coat and irritate his skin. Rinse out the soap and suds him up again. Rinse again. Make sure you get all the soap out. A bit of vinegar in the final rinse can help get out all the soap and restore the pH balance in the coat.

Be careful when you're bathing your dog not to get any shampoo in his eyes or ears. You can put a bit of cotton in his ears to keep water out, but most Corgis I know vigorously shake their heads until the cotton comes out. If you must wash the face, use a soft cloth and gently wipe away any dirt, using just water and no soap at all.

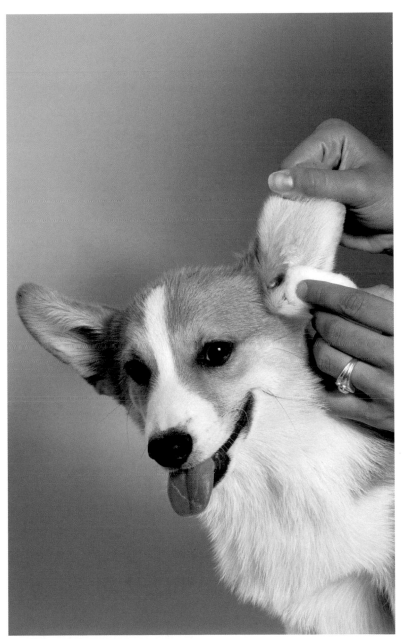

Your Pembroke Welsh Corgi's ears need to be kept clean at all times. Wipe the ears with a soft, damp cloth to remove any dirt and wax buildup.

Corgi ears usually stay fairly clean because they are open to the air, but there are special ear cleaners for dogs should you need them. Or again, a soft, wet cloth may be used. Don't push into the ear canal with anything! If there's an odor, discharge, or heavy wax buildup, or if your dog is scratching his ears, schedule a visit to your veterinarian for the proper treatment.

When you've finished the bath, use several towels to dry your Corgi. There are hair dryers designed especially for dogs, but if you've toweled him off well and he can stay inside until he's dry if it's cold out, then you should be fine.

Finally, when the coat is still damp, brush out all the hair that has been loosened by the bathing, and you're done.

COLD WEATHER CARE

Corgis have a wonderful double coat, which is not always so wonderful when your Corgi is shedding. However, it is a definite plus when your Corgi is outside. That double coat will keep your Corgi warm and dry in the pouring rain, snow, and cold. There's no need to buy a fancy coat for your Corgi. That's not to say you'll want to leave your Corgi outdoors all the time or with no shelter. No dog should be out without shelter, and if a Corgi is left unattended, the odds are he will get into some kind of mischief and probably start barking as well. Also, although Corgis are a hardy breed, they do best living with their people. If they are going to spend large blocks of time outdoors, make sure they have a sheltered area to get away from the weather.

Pay attention to your dog's ear tips and feet if you're planning an extended romp in the snow. Although a Corgi's ears are fairly well protected with fur, there is a chance of frostbite.

When your Corgi comes in from a romp in the snow, a quick, brisk rub with a towel will get rid of any snow that may have collected in his coat. Then check his feet for balls of snow or ice between the toes. Keeping the foot fur trimmed will help reduce this problem, and a bit of petroleum jelly will help protect his paws if you notice they're becoming dry or cracked. If you walk your Corgi on sidewalks or across streets, you'll definitely want to wipe off his feet when he comes in to get rid of any salt or de-icing products he may have walked through. Salt and de-icing chemicals may irritate his pads; if he licks his paws, the salt and chemicals may give him an upset stomach.

If you're trying to clear the ice off your own steps, consider a pet-safe de-icer. Or if you just want traction, spread some kitty litter on the steps. The drawback to the litter is that your dog may track it into the house.

HOT WEATHER CARE

In spite of their double coat, Corgis can cope with hot weather much better than breeds with shorter noses, but you still need to help them deal with summer's heat. First of all, always make sure your Corgi has plenty of

Corgis love to play in the snow. Just make sure that your dog doesn't stay out too long in cold weather. He may get frostbite.

clean, fresh water to drink. You'll notice your dog drinks much more in the summer than in the winter. Don't leave your dog out for long periods in a yard with no shade. Pay attention to the shade patterns in your yard. There is a period in the middle of the day when my yard offers very little shade. Watch to see what your yard is like because prolonged exposure to the sun can lead to heat stroke. With heat stroke, your dog may drool, stagger, or even collapse. Get him into the shade immediately. Use cool water to bring down his body temperature. Wet down his feet and ears, especially, and offer him water to drink. If your dog is unconscious, get him to your veterinarian immediately.

Your Corgi will still appreciate walks in the summer, but plan them for early morning or in the evening, when the air is cooler. You'll both enjoy a walk more when it's cooler, and you'll also avoid the risk of having your Corgi burn his paws on hot pavement.

If you're away during the day and your Corgi is indoors, make sure he has someplace cool to be. Kitchens and bathrooms usually have cool floors, or you might want to leave the door to the basement partially open for your Corgi. If you confine your dog to just one room when you are out, make sure it's a room that stays cool all day, not one with south or west-facing windows. If your dog is crated in a wire crate with a cover, flip up the cover so there's plenty of ventilation. Make sure it is in a permanently shady location. If your dog is apt to tip over the water dish, make sure the dish is securely anchored in some way. You might want to use a small bucket to ensure that your dog doesn't run out of water.

If left outside in warm weather, your dog will try to find a cool spot to relax. Always make sure that there is plenty of cool water and a good amount of shade or shelter when leaving your dog outside.

Indoors or out, most dogs enjoy the occasional ice cube when the weather is hot, and a few ice cubes added to the water dish helps keep that water cool.

Don't shave your Corgi for the summer. He needs that fur to protect his skin from sunburn and from insects. Make sure he's thoroughly brushed out so that he's not carrying around excess fur, but don't shave him.

Corgis are generally very healthy dogs and don't need much in the way of special care. With good food, proper shelter, exercise, a bit of grooming, and regular checkups at the veterinarian, your Corgi will more than pay you back, as he will be your affectionate companion for life.

TRAINING Your Corgi

HOUSETRAINING

Probably one of the first things you'll want to do once you get your puppy home is to train him to eliminate outdoors. Corgis train fairly quickly compared to some other breeds, and one of the best tools for this training is a crate. Dogs don't like to soil their own beds. Given a chance and within a reasonable time frame, a puppy will learn to hold it until he is taken to an appropriate spot. The other advantage to a crate is that it has a small, easy-to-clean surface, so if the puppy does have an accident in the crate, it is easier to clean than the rug and causes less damage.

There is more than one way to housetrain a puppy, but no matter what the method used, the key to success is consistency on your part and a schedule that a young puppy can reasonably meet. For instance, crating your puppy for eight hours straight is too long, and it is unreasonable to expect him to go that long without eliminating. If someone can't be available to take the puppy out at shorter

Potty training will be much easier for your Pembroke Welsh Corgi pup if you continually bring him back to the same spot to eliminate.

intervals, you'll have to start with paper training, layering a chosen room or corner of a room with papers and confining the puppy to that area. This will take longer but will work eventually.

First, let's discuss housetraining with a crate. Take the puppy out first thing in the morning. Open the crate, remove the puppy and head for the yard. Do not open the crate and coax the puppy to follow you through the house to the yard. The puppy is probably not going to make it that far. Carry him so that he goes in the yard in the spot you've chosen. The fewer mistakes that are made in the house, the faster the housetraining will be.

Praise your puppy when he goes in the right spot. Then take him in the house for breakfast, both his and yours. Keep him crated while you eat, just in case. Take him back out 20 to 30 minutes after he's eaten. Give him some playtime before everyone leaves for school or work. Take him out one more time and then put him back in his crate for no more than four hours. (If you can't get home for lunch, see if there's a neighbor who can help.) After this time has elapsed, take the puppy out immediately. There should also be another meal, some playtime, and another trip out, and then back in the crate. If you have children, this means that in another two or three hours someone will be home for another trip out and more playtime. Make sure everyone understands the importance of getting the puppy outdoors when he needs to relieve himself. Puppies typically sniff and circle, but they are also very quick, and with Corgi puppies, sometimes it's hard to tell if they're squatting or not.

After dinner, it's out again and another play session. Then, because puppies (like babies) need lots of sleep, your puppy may sleep during the evening while you're watching television. Take him out last time at about 11 p.m. If he's kept warm all night, he should make it until you are up at 6 to start the day. Puppies are a lot like people in that regard. If your puppy gets cold in the night, he'll wake up, and if he wakes up, he'll have to go. Having a crate in the bedroom means that not only does the puppy get to be with you, but if he wakes up and cries to go out, you'll hear him right away.

Suppose you have no neighbors or children and can't get away regularly at noon. In this case, you should consider paper training. Choose a room for confining the puppy. It could be your kitchen, bathroom, or laundry room. If the room is too large to easily cover

Familiarize yourself with the telltale signs that your pup needs to be taken outside to eliminate.

the floor with newspapers, you can block off a section. Put the puppy's crate and toys and water bowl in the chosen area. When you are home, try to follow the schedule as discussed under using the crate. Take the puppy out after naps, after meals, and after playtime. When unattended, place the puppy in the papered area. When you clean up, remove the top layers of paper and replace with fresh paper. After a week or so, reduce the area covered by paper. If the puppy successfully uses the paper and not the uncovered floor, reduce the area even more. Continue until all the papers have been picked up.

A relatively new approach is puppy litter. Just like a cat, you can teach your dog to use a litter pan filled with special litter. While this may not be practical for an adult Corgi, it might be just the thing as an interim step, like the newspapers. Remember, whatever method you use, be patient and be consistent.

Housetraining may take until the puppy is 12 to 16 weeks old or possibly longer, depending on the puppy, but it's not something that can be rushed. Also, even if your puppy seems reliable at 16 weeks, there may be lapses. If someone is home with the puppy, he can probably have the run of the house, but if you're going out, don't leave the puppy loose. Take the precaution of putting him in his crate or in a safe room. Besides the possibility of an accident, puppies love to chew. Don't give him the chance to chew the fringe of the Oriental rug, the rung of a chair, or worse yet, an electrical cord.

INFORMAL OBEDIENCE

While it is not a good idea to start formal training or even puppy classes until your dog has had all his vaccinations, you can start some simple training at home. Most Corgis are chowhounds and can be motivated by food, especially soft treats. Just remember that the piece you offer doesn't have to be very large. Keep your training sessions short and happy. Three or four short sessions of five minutes each are more effective than one session of 20 minutes, especially with a puppy.

Come

While you won't be doing formal recalls, the puppy should know his name and should come when called. Offer treats and call your puppy. Sound happy and excited. If his attention wanders, run

Every dog has the right to be trained. Teach your Pembroke Welsh Corgi exactly which behaviors are tolerated and which ones are not.

away from your puppy, calling his name. When he comes, give him a treat and praise him. Never call your puppy for punishment or for something he may find unpleasant. Call him to dinner, not to show him an accident on the rug. If it's time to do his nails, go and get him and pick him up. No matter how frustrated the puppy may make you when you're in a hurry and he won't come in, when you do get him, be gentle and praise him. He must always associate good things with obeying the come command.

Stay

Next, you might want to teach your Corgi to stay. Start with your Corgi sitting on your left. Place your open palm in front of his nose and give the stay command. Take one step directly in front of the Corgi. Move back beside him, and praise. Gradually extend the amount of time you are in front of him before you release him. As he seems to understand the command, move backward a step or two. Again, keep lessons short and happy, and always end on a positive note.

Sit

Sitting is probably the easiest thing you can teach a puppy. Hold a treat in front of the dog and slowly move it back over the top of his head. Don't hold it too high or he'll be tempted to jump up. As the treat moves back, give the sit command. The puppy will sit as he tries to follow the treat with his eyes and nose. The instant he sits, give him the treat and tell him how wonderful he is.

Down

Down is a little harder. Many books and instructors will tell you that once your dog is sitting, you should just take a treat and slowly move it down toward his feet and out a bit. The dog will slide into the down. I've seen this work with many other breeds, but most Corgis pop right up onto all four feet. I don't know if it's the short legs or what, but Corgis generally lean forward after the treat and their hindquarters go up.

One of the best ways to teach down to a Corgi is to teach him a few other commands first, so he understands the concept of learning something. Teach him a sit. Teach a stay. Teach him to walk nicely, even if you won't ever require a perfect heel position. Then, try a down. Tell your Corgi to sit. Hold a treat in your hand, move it slowly down and away, and give the command to down. The Corgi will likely pop up to all fours and go after the hand holding the treat. Don't let him get the treat. He may paw at your hand or even nibble at it, trying to get the treat. He may sit again. Be patient. Eventually, he will lie down, and that's when you should quickly give him the treat and praise him.

Other Lessons

Since most Corgis love to retrieve, name the actions as you play with your Corgi. Throw the ball and tell him to "fetch," or "take it." When he brings it back, tell him to "leave it," or "drop it." Work on having him put it in your hand. I teach my Corgis to "leave it" with almost everything. If there's 3 feet of snow in the backyard and a Corgi has a toy in his mouth, I want it left indoors. I don't want to have to dig through the snow to find it or let it stay hidden until spring. Also, if one of the dogs happens to find a dead critter and

One of the easiest commands to teach your Pembroke Welsh Corgi is to sit. Most dogs will master it very quickly.

Your Pembroke Welsh Corgi must be taught that commands must be followed. Never give a command that you are not willing or able to enforce.

decides he'd like to bring it indoors, I don't want to have to pry it from his jaws. I want him to leave it.

Clicker Training

Clicker training has become very popular and is a good way to train your puppy using only positive methods. The training clickers are available at most pet supply stores, or you can even use a ballpoint pen for the clicker sound. The important thing is the timing with a clicker. Whenever your puppy does something you want him to do, click and treat. The clicker marks the behavior at the instant it occurs. There's no delay as there might be with a word of praise and a treat. Get your puppy used to the idea that when he hears the click, he will get a treat. Click and treat several times so the puppy makes the connection between clicker and treat. This won't take long.

Then, when your puppy starts to sit, for instance, click and treat. The thing to remember about clicker training is that you must click as you get the behavior. It may take a little practice to get your timing right. Also, with clicker training, there is no coercion at all. There is no pressure on the neck, shoulders, or rump, and there's no positioning of the legs or body.

If you've got an instructor in your area who uses clicker training, talk to him or her about how best to use it. Read a book or two on the subject. It may take you awhile to learn it yourself, but it will work, and it won't take your Corgi long to understand it. Besides basic obedience, clicker training can be used in agility training, as well as almost any other area of dog training.

No matter what method or combination of methods you use to train your Corgi, remember to keep sessions short and positive. Two or three 10-minute sessions are better than one long session. Patience is also important. Don't lose your temper with your puppy. With Corgis, a sense of humor also helps.

ACTIVITIES AND EVENTS FOR YOU AND YOUR DOG

Canine Good Citizen®

Beyond basic good manners and a few simple obedience commands, you might want to think about getting a CGC® title on your dog. CGC® stands for Canine Good Citizen® and it is a title awarded by the American Kennel Club to any dog passing a test given by a certified tester. There are ten different steps to the test. You dog must allow a stranger to approach, and he must sit quietly and allow the person to pet him. He must allow someone to groom him. You supply the brush or comb and someone runs it lightly over your Corgi's body. You'll be required to walk your dog on a loose lead through a crowd of people. Next, you will be asked to put your dog on first a sit and then a down. You must also leave your dog, and he must stay until you call him.

Your dog will also be tested on how he reacts to distractions. Since many people who have their dog tested for the CGC® are also interested in therapy dog work, the distractions are frequently wheelchairs, a person on crutches, or a person using a walker. The crutches may be thrown to the ground, or the walker may be knocked over to see how well your dog recovers from being startled. Finally, you must tie your dog or hand him to someone to hold and go out of sight for three minutes. Your dog may move about, but must not whine, bark, or pull to go after you. If you have taken any obedience lessons at all, your dog should be able to pass the CGC® test.

Obedience

If your dog passes the CGC® test or you have been enjoying obedience classes, you may want to consider earning obedience titles. Corgis learn quickly and make wonderful obedience dogs. They can also be very creative, adding their own interpretation to the exercises. If you have not been taking formal classes, you may want to consider them if you are going to compete in formal obedience trials. An instructor will know the best way to teach specific exercises, and attending class will get your dog used to other dogs. Also, when practicing the long sits and downs, it is better to do them in a group as it simulates actual trial conditions.

Companion Dog (CD)

The first obedience degree is the Companion Dog title (CD). To be awarded a CD, your dog must qualify under three different judges. A qualifying score is 170 out of a possible 200 points. Also, your dog must win at least half of the points awarded for each exercise. The exercises your dog must pass are: heel on lead and figure eight (40 points), stand for examination (30 points), heel off lead (40 points), the recall (30 points), long sit (30 points), and the long down (30 points).

Training your Pembroke Welsh Corgi for the Canine Good Citizen® Test will ensure that he has good manners and will be welcomed anywhere.

For heeling on lead, the judge will call out instructions, such as right turn, fast, slow, normal, and halt, and you and your dog must follow these commands, with your dog remaining always in a heel position. The figure eight consists of walking with your dog in a figure eight pattern around two stewards. On the stand for examination, you remove your lead, command your dog to stand and stay, and move 6 feet away while the judge lightly touches your dog. Then you return to the dog's side.

Heel free is just what it sounds like; you again follow the judge's directions, only this time your Corgi is off lead. For the recall, you will place your Corgi on a sit stay and walk about 35 feet from your dog, then turn to face him. At the judge's signal, you will call your dog, and he should move rapidly to sit in front of you. At another signal from the judge, you will command your dog to move into the heel position.

The group exercises are the long sit and the long down. The long sit lasts for one minute, the long down for three. In both of these exercises, competitors line up with their dogs. Armbands and leads are placed behind the dogs. At the command from the judge, you place your dog in either the sit or down and walk to the far side of the ring, turn, and face your dog. Your dog must remain in either the sit or down position, depending on which position the exercise calls for, until you have returned to his side and the judge has ended the exercise with the words, "exercise finished."

The group exercises are one of the reasons a class situation is helpful. Besides getting your dog used to other dogs, your instructor may introduce distractions to *proof* your dog. If you dog can handle classroom distractions without breaking his sit or stay, the odds are he will remain in position in the ring.

Companion Dog Excellent (CDX)

If you and your dog work well as a team and you both enjoy practicing as well as competing, it shouldn't take long to get your CD. Then it's time to try for a Companion Dog Excellent title (CDX). Once again, you must qualify under three different judges, and once again a qualifying score is 170 out of 200, but for a CDX, the exercises change. You will still be asked to follow a heeling pattern and do a figure eight, but this time, it's all off lead for 40 points. There is another recall, but this time, as your dog moves toward you, at the judge's signal, you must command your dog to down. At another signal, you recall your dog, and he continues in to sit in front of you. This is the drop on recall and is worth 30 points.

The long sits and downs are longer, with the sit being for three minutes and the down being for five; after you have positioned your dog and walked away, you are led out of the ring and out of sight for the required time. The long sit and the long down are each worth 30 points.

To earn a CDX, your dog must also retrieve and jump. Dog supply stores and catalogs will have just the right size dumbbell for your Corgi. During the trial, your dog must retrieve on the flat for 20 points, and retrieve over a high jump for 30 points. The jump height is based on the height of your dog at the withers. Corgis usually jump 12 inches. The other required jump is the broad jump, which is twice as long as the height of the high jump. If your Corgi jumps a high jump of 12 inches, he will need to jump a broad jump that is 24 inches long. The broad jump is worth 20 points. Again, class work may be just the thing. Teaching your dog to jump consistently should be taught slowly. Corgis are active dogs and may easily jump higher to get on the couch or into your lap, but formal training should start with a very low jump, getting your dog used to jumping on command. Pushing your dog can lead to injury and may make him refuse to jump at all.

Utility Dog (UD)

Competition for Utility Dog (UD) changes drastically. Classes no longer include long sits and downs. There is a heeling pattern to follow, but this time there are no verbal commands. All commands must be hand signals. Included in this exercise is the command to stand your dog, leave your dog, and at the judge's signals, to drop (or down) your dog, sit, come, and finish (return to heel position), all with hand signals. This is the signal exercise and is worth 40 points.

Next comes scent discrimination. In scent discrimination, your dog is asked to select the article with your scent on it. Scent articles come in sets of two, with one set being entirely metal and one set being leather. Each article is numbered. Although technically they may be of any shape, the articles are usually small dumbbells in the appropriate material, which makes it easier for the dog to pick up. During a trial, the judge will indicate which number article in each set will be used. These two articles are set aside. The remaining eight articles are placed on the ground about 20 feet from you and your dog. With your back to the articles, you will then place your scent on either the metal or leather article, using your hands. Without touching the article, the judge will then take it, either on his clipboard, or with tongs, and place it with the other articles on the ground. At the signal, you and your dog will turn to face the articles, and you will send your dog to retrieve the article you have handled. The process is repeated with the next article.

The next exercise is the directed retrieve. In this exercise, while you and your dog have your back to the steward, he or she drops three white gloves in a line. The judge then has you turn to face the gloves, and once you are turned, indicates which glove your dog is to retrieve.

Sets of three Corgi-sized gloves may be purchased from catalogs or booths at dog shows, so you don't need to worry about your Corgi tripping on a huge work glove or about buying two pairs of gloves and throwing one glove away.

The next exercise is the moving stand and examination. In this exercise, the dog heels beside you until the judge gives you the command to stand your dog. At this point, without stopping, you command your dog to stand while you continue another 10 to 12 feet and then turn and face your dog. The judge examines your dog, and then you call the dog to heel.

The directed jump has two jumps: the high jump, such as is used in CDX competition, and the bar jump, which is a single bar supported by two uprights. In this exercise, you send the dog away from you to the far side of the ring. At the command to sit, your dog will turn to face you and sit. When the judge indicates either *high* or *bar* jump, you give a signal, and your dog must jump the designated jump. This is then repeated for the second jump.

Utility Dog Excellent is the next title up the obedience ladder and may be earned by achieving a qualifying score in both Open B and Utility B classes at ten separate approved events.

Obedience Trial Champion (OTCH)

Ready for still more obedience? Then you're ready to try for an obedience trial championship, or OTCH. To put an OTCH on your dog, you must win 100 points from either the Open B or Utility B class. Points are based on the number of dogs you beat. You can only win points if you are in first or second place in your class. In addition, you must, under three different judges, win a first place in Open B over six dogs or more, a first in Utility B over three dogs or more, and another first in either class, under the listed conditions.

If obedience sounds just right for you and your Corgi, get the booklet of official regulations from the AKC, find an instructor you like, and enjoy!

Agility

If you can barely get your dog to heel, or obedience just doesn't sound like your cup of tea, don't worry; there are lots of other things you can do with your Corgi! You might want to try agility. Agility is a rapidly growing sport that gives both you and your dog exercise and fun. Again, it's a good idea to find a class and a good instructor. Agility equipment takes up a lot of room and is fairly expensive to purchase, although if you are at all handy, you can build most of it yourself.

Agility is gaining popularity in the US. Pembroke Welsh Corgis have been known to excel at agility.

If you are interested in agility, there are three major organizations: the AKC, the United States Dog Agility Association (USDAA), and the North American Dog Agility Council (NADAC). Each has its own set of rules and regulations. Talk to other people in the sport, and contact the organizations for their rules and regulations, as each organization has slightly different rules, and these rules change periodically.

Each organization has three levels of competition. The AKC has Novice, Open, and Excellent. USDAA has Starters/Novice, Advanced, and Master. NADAC has Novice, Open, and Elite. The AKC also has Jumpers with Weaves (JWW), which is a course with no contact obstacles. It has jumps, weave poles, and may or may not have open and/or closed tunnels. Titles in JWW include Novice, Open, Excellent, and Master Excellent. You can also go on to win agility championships.

If you are serious about competing in agility, make sure you have a current set of rules and regulations for whatever organization you will be competing in, as the regulations do differ. Take refusals as an example. A refusal is when a dog hesitates or refuses before performing an obstacle or if he "runs out" or "runs by" and has to circle back to approach the obstacle again. With the AKC, all refusals are judged at every level, but you can still qualify in Novice with two refusals and in Open with one refusal. No refusals are allowed at the Excellent level.

NADAC does not judge refusals at any level since the time wasted will probably prevent the dog from qualifying anyway. With the USDAA, refusals are not judged at the Novice level, are only judged for the contact obstacles at the Advanced level and the weave poles, and are judged at all obstacles at the Master level.

The main obstacles in an agility course are the A-frame, where the dog goes up one side of the *A* and down the other; the dog walk, which is a sloping board that leads up to another level board across which the dog walks and then another sloping board down to the ground; a seesaw; four types of jumps—broad, panel, bar, and tire or window jumps; a pause table, where you must, at the judge's direction, either sit or down your dog for the count of five; an open tunnel; and a closed tunnel, or chute, which consists of an open, rigid entry area, and an expanse of cloth for the exit. The fabric has no support, so the dog must push through it to exit. Weave poles are the final element, and are not a part of an AKC novice course.

The A-frame, the dog walk, and the seesaw are all *contact obstacles*; that is, they all have a *contact zone* where the obstacle touches the ground, and it is usually painted yellow. The dog must touch this area as he gets both on and off of the obstacle. This is to ensure that the dog does not leap on or off the obstacle, thus risking injury.

Agility is a very challenging and complex sport, but as your dog gains confidence, he will perform with almost the same speed that he chases a ball. This speed can be a problem at advanced levels because the dog may miss the yellow contact zone coming off an obstacle. The best advice is to put in the time at the Novice level, making sure you get a solid contact so that this does not become a problem at advanced levels. It's also a good idea to wait a bit and not push the dog too hard. A dog may not compete until he is 12 months old, and it is a good idea to wait until he is 18 months to 2 years old before actually competing. This gives both you and your dog time to get in condition and build up stamina.

If you plan to do agility, the weave poles are an obstacle you will definitely want to have in your own backyard. For competitive agility, one class a week is not enough to teach your dog proficiency on the weave poles. A few jumps are also a good idea. Agility competitor and judge Anne Platt says that although Corgis can easily jump 12 inches, they frequently knock jump bars down. She is not sure if this is because it doesn't bother them or if it is because when they are running full speed, they tend to flatten out and so don't get their legs high enough. Either way, taking jumps at full speed is something you'll want to practice if you plan to compete in agility.

Tracking

Tracking is another activity that you can enjoy with your Corgi. You will need a harness and a tracking lead, which must be between 20 and 40 feet long. You will also need access to some wide-open spaces for laying tracks.

Tracking tests a dog's ability at following a particular scent over various terrains. Variable Surface Tracking (VST) includes pavement as well as other surfaces, such as gravel and grass. As with obedience titles, there are various levels of tracking. Each level is determined by the number of turns in the trail, the length of the trail, and how long it has *aged* before the dog starts the trail. *Aging* refers to the amount of time between when the trail is laid and the time when the dog is allowed to start tracking. Tracking titles are Tracking Dog (TD), Tracking Dog Excellent (TDX) and Variable Surface Tracking (VST).

When training, take care that the trail is not crossed or otherwise contaminated by scents other than that of the tracklayer. To begin training, the handler makes a simple trail, crushing the grass and placing a piece of hot dog in each footprint. This marks the trail in three ways: handler scent, crushed vegetation, and hot dog. At the end of the trail, place something the dog will be happy to find. A glove containing more hot dog is a common item, but it could be the dog's favorite toy. Gradually, trails get longer, include turns, and are aged.

Tracking Dog (TD)

To earn the TD title, your dog must follow a track that is at least 440 yards long, has three to five turns, and has been aged at least 30 minutes and no longer than 2 hours. The track can't cross any paved area or any body of water, and there are two starting flags, one 30 yards from the first, to indicate the direction in which the track was laid. At the end of the track is either a glove or wallet, which the dog must indicate in some way.

Tracking Dog Excellent (TDX)

For the TDX title, the track increases to at least 800 yards long, has five to seven turns, and has been aged at least three hours and no more than five. For this title, there are four articles to be found along the trail, with only the last one being a glove or wallet, and two *cross tracks* are laid, trails that cross the main track. There must also be two obstacles in a TDX track. An obstacle may be a stream, a fence, a bridge, a lightly traveled road, or a gully. These obstacles test the dog's ability to continue scenting under different physical and handling conditions, all while overcoming a physical obstacle. The handler is allowed to assist the dog over or under obstacles. With a Corgi's short legs, this may indeed be necessary.

Variable Surface Tracking (VST)

VST tracking tests your Corgi's ability to track over changing surfaces. A dog must already have a TD or a TDX title to compete for a VST. In this test, the trail must cross three different surfaces, with one being vegetation and the other two a combination of

Most dogs are good at following their noses. This little Corgi smells something interesting around this stump.

concrete, asphalt, gravel, sand, hardpan, or mulch. The track is aged for three to five hours and must have between four and eight turns. Besides adding to the complexity with different surfaces, tracks should be laid near buildings, which can change the pattern of the scent. Trails may not, however, lead through any building with closed doors and sides. As with the TDX, there are four articles to be found, but the requirements for these articles are much more exact for the VST. To quote from the AKC booklet on tracking regulations, "Each article shall not be smaller than 2" x 5" nor larger than 5" x 5" and shall weigh no more than 8 ounces. There shall be one leather, one plastic (rigid or semi-rigid), one metal, and one fabric article, which shall be handled by the Tracklayer and are to be dropped on the track by the Tracklayer at the points indicated on the judges' charts. The first article shall be fabric or leather. The last article shall be clearly marked with the number 4."

To complete a tracking title, two judges must certify that the dog has successfully completed the track for any given trail. A Champion

Tracker title (CT) is awarded to any dog that has earned all three tracking titles.

Corgis enjoy tracking, but their size can be a bit of a drawback if there is a fallen tree to scramble over. Going around an obstacle may mean losing the scent, so keep that in mind as you work with your dog.

As with any of the performance events, get a copy of the AKC regulations. You can learn to track by yourself, but if you can find someone to help you who is experienced in tracking, it will speed the process and prevent mistakes. It's always easier to learn it the right way first, rather than have to correct training errors.

Herding

The Corgi is a member of the herding group and so may earn a herding title from the American Kennel Club. Your Corgi may also compete in events sponsored by the American Herding Breeds Association (AHBA).

Before trying to find a trainer or actually working toward a title, see if you can find someone who has stock and does herding. Try your Corgi with some ducks or sheep to see if he does indeed have an instinct to herd. If your dog has never been around any kind of stock, he may be so interested in the new sights and smells that even if he does have the herding instinct, it will not be evident. You may need to try him on stock three or four times before anything happens.

A woman I met at a herding test had entered her Corgi but didn't have much hope. She'd taken him to see sheep at a county fair and he had hidden behind her legs. As if to make up for that, when he was let loose at the test, he herded like he'd been doing it all his life.

The AKC offers five herding titles, as well as a herding championship. Dogs may earn a Herding Test (HT), a Pre-Trial Test (PT), and in trial classes, Herding Started (HS), Herding Intermediate (HI), and Herding Excellent (HX) for those dogs that have successfully completed the Herding Advanced course three times under three different judges. The Herding Championship (HC) is awarded to dogs that have earned their HX and have then gone on to win at least 15 championship points in Advanced classes. Points are awarded based on how many dogs competed, and they are awarded to dogs in first, second, third, or fourth place, depending on the size of the entry.

Corgis make great herding dogs. These Corgis and their Golden Retriever friend make a great team.

The Herding Test and the Pre-Trial Test are indeed tests, with both being much less rigorous than the trials. You do not, however, need to compete or earn a test title before entering trials. This should depend on how ready you and your dog are. Herding is growing in popularity, but you still may need to drive quite a distance to find an instructor. Remember, you need to practice with animals that are accustomed to being worked; you can't just find a flock of sheep and turn your dog loose.

You may enter a dog as young as nine months in any AKC herding test or trial.

The AHBA offers a *test* program, which includes two titles to be earned, both on a pass/fail basis. The test is called the Herding Capability Test, where the dog may be tested on sheep, goats, ducks, geese, or cattle. The dog must pass under two different judges, and the second leg requires more skill. Junior Herding Dog has a simple course through which the stock is taken. If your Corgi really shows promise and you enjoy herding, you can go for a Herding Trial Dog or Herding Ranch Dog title. Each of these titles has three levels of difficulty, and the dog must receive a qualifying score under two different judges. The AHBA also offers a Herding Trial Championship, which is earned by obtaining ten additional qualifying scores in advanced classes.

Therapy Dog

If your own tendencies lean more toward couch potato than athlete, maybe therapy work is the niche for you and your Corgi. Visiting a nursing home doesn't require much physical effort, but the emotional rewards can be tremendous. This is a chance for you to share your wonderful dog with people whose activities have become limited.

There are organizations that register therapy dogs, among them Therapy Dogs International and the Delta Society. Actually having a registered therapy dog means that your dog has passed a test similar to the Canine Good Citizen® test, with the addition of testing your dog around someone in a wheelchair and someone using a walker or crutches or both. The person using the walker or

Therapy dogs can help brighten someone's day. If your dog is well mannered and loves people, he may make a great therapy dog.

crutches will usually drop them, testing your dog's reaction to strange noises and also to the walker and crutches themselves. If your dog becomes a *registered* therapy dog, he will have a special ID tag for his collar and may have a laminated wallet card that you can show. The registering agency will need proof that your dog passed the necessary test and that all vaccinations are up to date. The agency may provide insurance coverage for visits and will offer guidelines for taking your dog to hospitals or other health care facilities.

Your dog doesn't need to be registered to make visits, but it's a good idea to follow many of the guidelines, including checking to see how your dog will react to wheelchairs and walkers *before* you make a visit. Take proof of vaccinations with you when you visit, and make sure your dog is well groomed and has had his nails trimmed.

Corgis make good therapy dogs because their size is not threatening. A drawback is that they are a bit hard to reach for petting when a person is in a wheelchair or a bed, but you can easily pick up your dog and hold him so that he can receive the loving attention of those you are visiting.

Your dog may or may not be permitted into a person's lap or onto a bed. Check with the facility manager *before* you allow either of these behaviors. Older people have more delicate skin, and there may be a concern that the dog's nails will bruise or tear the skin.

If you and your dog enjoy visiting and want to spread the word about proper dog care, consider visiting Scout troop meetings, Sunday schools, or day care classes. Of course, as with health care facilities, be confident that your dog is comfortable around children so that the visit is a happy experience for everyone.

The Conformation Ring

Conformation judging is what most people think of when they think of a dog show. The Group and Best in Show judging is what you see on television when a show such as the Westminster Kennel Club dog show is televised. Dog shows are held year round, indoors and out, and may range in size from entries of under a hundred to over three thousand. In the early years of dog shows, all the shows were benched; that is, all dogs of the same breed were together in the benching area, and were there all day. Today, there are only six benched shows left in the country. All other shows are unbenched, which means you can arrive at any time before your dog is to be judged and may leave as soon as the judging is finished.

For people who need to drive back and forth, this type of show can save on hotel bills and meals, but it isn't as easy to find someone to talk to if you want to research a breed of dog. At benched shows, the dog must remain on his bench for the hours of the show, unless the dog is being groomed, exercised, fed, or shown. The Westminster Kennel Club show is benched. It is one of the most prestigious shows in the country, and entries usually close within minutes of them opening. Because of the space restrictions, only 2,500 dogs may enter this show, and it is now open only to champions.

You might not have thought much about showing your Corgi when you got him, but chances are your breeder discussed with you whether or not your puppy was potentially show quality. Show quality means your dog has no disqualifying faults as discussed in the standard, and that he is structurally sound and built as a Corgi should be. If you think you might enjoy showing him, ask your breeder or someone who knows Corgis to re-evaluate him. If their opinion is positive, give it a try!

As with other dog-related activities, it is possible to learn from books and from trial and error, but it is much, much easier if you can find someone to help you. A dog show mentor can save you time and money and may mean the difference between giving up and persevering.

Many kennel clubs offer handling classes, and this an excellent place to learn about how to gait and stack your dog and what kind of collar, lead, and bait to use With my first show dog, I had both a mentor, in the breeder of the dog, and I also attended classes in handling. The formal class gave my dog socialization with other dogs, and I received pointers on how to place my dog on the table (the Corgi is a "table breed"; the judge examines him on a grooming table, as well as watches him move and stand on the ground), move at the proper pace, and learn the different patterns of movement that the judge might request. (In order to see your dog in action, the judge may ask for a "down and back," a "triangle," or an "L." You'll want to practice these before you actually show your dog.)

Whether or not you attend formal classes, you may want to attend a match or two before you actually enter a show. A match is an event put on by a dog club. It is run like a dog show, but the dogs can't win any points. It is frequently more casual than a show, and

If you plan on showing your Corgi, make sure that you have properly trained him for the show ring.

a judge at a match is more likely to give you advice than is a judge at a licensed show. Match entry fees are also much less than those of a show.

When I first started showing, my mentor gave me breed-specific tips in terms of what kind of collar and lead work best, a good speed at which to move for gaiting, and ideas for bait, the food used to get a dog's attention in the ring. My mentor showed me how to groom for the ring and also helped me with entry forms and suggested judges who might like my dog. This last tip can definitely help you save time and money. An experienced dog show competitor keeps a file on judges and what they may or may not like in a particular dog. If your dog's movement is not the best, there's no point in showing to a judge who considers movement very important. If your dog's head fits the standard in every way, there is probably a judge who is looking for just that feature.

Another advantage to having a mentor is that you and he or she can travel together to your first few shows. It's a lot less intimidating when you are traveling with someone who knows where to go and what to do.

Let's pretend to do just that...go to a show. You've purchased the proper show lead as recommended by your mentor, and you've attended classes so you understand how to move your dog at the correct pace around the ring and how to stack your dog on the table so the judge can examine him. You've cooked hot dogs or liver or chicken, or whatever treats your dog loves so that you can get his attention in the ring. Your dog is also in good show condition, that is, well groomed and in coat. If your dog is out of coat, there is probably no point in showing. Show condition also means that your dog is ready in the physical sense; he is not soft and flabby, but has gotten regular daily exercise to give him good muscle tone.

Supplies

It's time to pack the car for the show. The most important item, of course, is your dog. But how is he to travel? You'll need his crate in the car, and you may want an extra one for your hotel room and maybe even one at the show site. Pack your tack box, which holds all your grooming supplies. Brushes, treats, show leads, spray bottles of water, baby wipes, waterless shampoo, whatever you need to make sure your dog looks his best for the judge. You'll need your grooming table, too, and a grooming smock, and don't forget extra towels. You'll want one for on the grooming table, one for wiping off mud, drying feet, (maybe drying the entire dog if it rains), a couple for extra bedding in case what is in the crate gets dirty—you can never have too many towels. A wire exercise pen is a good idea, too, so your Corgi has a place other than his crate to move around in. In addition, if the grounds are muddy or very crowded, he will have a place for elimination without the need for a walk. Water is essential. Carry your own water from home to prevent any digestive upset. You'll also want to take food, of course, if you are going for more than the day. You may want to carry some for yourself, as well as some for the dog. Dog show food is usually of the hot dog and hamburger variety, if it exists at all. A small cooler packed with some sandwiches or snacks can make your day more pleasant.

What to Wear

Consider your wardrobe as you pack. You want to look neat and well groomed, but you should also be prepared for whatever weather you may encounter. At an indoor show, this isn't such a concern, but at an outdoor show, you may encounter heat, cold, rain, mud, and/or wind. Follow the Scout motto and be prepared. Throw your raincoat in the car, no matter what the long-range weather forecast says. Carry extra shoes and a hat. Flat, comfortable shoes are a must for both men and women; you don't want to risk falling in the ring, and, you're going to be on your feet for most of the day, so you don't want them to be tired. Men should wear a sport coat and tie; women should wear a dress or skirt, although a pants suit is acceptable. Skirts should be loose enough to move freely in, without being too full. A billowing skirt can obscure the judges' view of your dog and may even interrupt your dog's gait if the skirt blows across his face. Solid colors that make a good contrasting background to your dog are an excellent choice.

Paperwork

Don't forget your paperwork. Always carry your dog's current rabies certificate. I make a copy and keep it in my tack box. You'll also want your judging schedule so you'll know where you're supposed to be and at what time, as well as your dog's entry form, which is usually your ticket to enter the show. Remember to take any directions you need to get to the show site, and allow yourself plenty of time to get there. You've paid to enter your dog in the show; make sure you don't miss your ring time.

Arrival

You've made your list, checked it twice, and the car is loaded and ready to go. If you are going to an indoor show, there will usually be an unloading area near a building door. You can unload your grooming table and supplies and then move your car to the parking area. It is a good idea to get to the show site early because grooming space fills up fast. Luckily, Corgis don't take up much room! At an outdoor show, the grooming area will usually be under a separate tent. Again, there will be a loading and unloading area. If the show site offers large, grassy parking areas with shade, you might want to simply set up your table next to your car; you can work out of your car and avoid unloading everything.

If you decide on this method, make sure you have some sort of awning or sunscreen to keep the car cool. Draping space blankets over the windows keeps out a lot of heat. Never, never, never leave your dog unattended in a closed car. Dogs do not perspire like humans do. Their lungs act as a cooling agent. If they are breathing in super hot air, there is no chance for the proper heat exchange, and they will quickly overheat.

Once you're settled, indoors or out, double check your judging time, find your ring so you know exactly where you'll be going, and if it's not too early, pick up your armband from the ring steward. Your armband number is on your entry form; just tell the steward your breed and the number. There will be rubber bands available so you can secure the band to your upper left arm.

Grooming

The next thing to do is to groom your dog. You should have already clipped your dog's toenails and foot fur at home and given him a bath if needed. Show site grooming for a Corgi should be a matter of touch up. Brush and comb thoroughly. If the site is muddy or wet, use waterless shampoo to spot clean. Wipe his feet. You may want to use powder or cornstarch to clean white feet. Check your dog's eyes, nose, and ears.

Next, you may want to crate your dog until just before you go to the ring, or you may want to head for your ring early. Some dogs show better if they go directly from their crate to the ring; others do better if they have a little time to settle down and get used to the crowd before showing. Experience will tell you. Either way, with or without your dog, try to watch the judge as he or she judges a few dogs so that you'll be ready for whatever pattern will be used when you gait your dog. Does the judge ask for the first dog to be put directly on the table, or will he or she ask you to go around the ring first? Knowing ahead of time will save time in the ring, and you'll be calmer, which will help both you and your dog.

Choosing a Class

Now, what class did you and your mentor decide was the best for your dog? Class choices are Puppy 6 -9 months, Puppy 9-12 months, 12-18 months, Novice, American Bred, Bred-by-Exhibitor, and Open. Entrants in the Novice class may not have any points, may not have won more than three first place ribbons from the Novice class, or may not have won a first place in any other class, except puppy. American Bred means the entered dog must have been bred in the United States. In the Bred-by-Exhibitor class, the owner or co-owner must have bred the dog or be a member of the immediate family. Any dog may be entered in the Open class. All classes are divided, with males competing against males and females competing against females.

Ribbons are awarded for first through fourth place. The winners of each class, those dogs that won the blue ribbon, then compete with other class winners for Winners Dog or Winners Bitch. The dog that wins here is the dog that earns one or more points towards a championship.

The Winners Dog and Winners Bitch then go on to compete with any champions entered for the title of Best of Breed. Should either of the winners go Best of Breed, they may also win more points. For instance, there may be enough dogs entered to give the Winners Dog three points, but only enough bitches entered to give the Winners Bitch two points. If the bitch should beat the male by going Best of Breed, then she would also receive three points. The point schedule which determines how many dogs you must beat for how many points is broken up into regions, and the show catalog will list this for each breed. To win three, four, or five points is to get a major. A championship is achieved with a total of not less than 15 points, of which the dog must win two majors under two different judges.

Even if your dog doesn't win, you'll want to watch the entire Corgi judging and cheer on the Best of Breed winner when he competes in the group ring. There are seven groups, and the Best of Breed winners from all of the entered breeds compete with others of their group. Corgis are in the Herding Group. The seven group winners then compete for the title of Best in Show.

Another part of most conformation shows is Junior Showmanship. This is a special class, designed to give younger dog lovers a chance to practice their handling skills. Classes are Novice, for those juniors who have not won three first place awards, with competition present, in a Novice Class, and Open, for those who have won three first place awards, with competition present, in a Novice Class. Usually, these two classes are further divided into Junior and Senior classes. Junior classes are for boys and girls who are at least 10 years old and under 14 years old on the day of the show. Senior class is for boys and girls who are at least 14 years old and under 18 years old on the day of the show. The dog being shown must belong to the Junior or to a member of his or her immediate family and must be eligible to be shown in regular conformation or obedience classes. Bitches in season may not be shown.

While conformation showing requires a dog to be registered with the AKC and to be intact, that is, not spayed or neutered, the competition events permit spayed or neutered dogs to compete. You may also compete with an unregistered dog, as long as you have an ILP number. ILP stands for Indefinite Listing Privilege. This number is granted to dogs that are purebred but that were never formally registered for whatever reason. You must submit pictures of your dog to the AKC, and if they agree the dog is the breed you say it is, you will be given an ILP number and be permitted to compete in performance events.

Corgis are such versatile little dogs that no matter what sport you choose, your Corgi will be a willing and competitive partner. If none of these dog sports appeals to you, don't worry. Your Corgi will be just as happy with regular walks and the occasional game of fetch.

HEALTH CARE

As mentioned earlier, there are certain basic vaccinations that your puppy should have. Combination vaccinations generally include distemper, leptospirosis, hepatitis, parvovirus, and may or may not also include parainfluenza. Your veterinarian may also recommend shots against Lyme disease or coronavirus. An inoculation against rabies is required in every state, but the time span between shots may differ. Some states require a rabies shot every year, some every three years. Check with your veterinarian for your state's requirements.

RABIES

Rabies is a virus that attacks the central nervous system of mammals and is spread through saliva. Common carriers in the wild include bats, foxes, raccoons, and skunks. Although there have been a few documented cases of survivors, rabies is considered a fatal disease. Once symptoms appear, there is no cure. Rabies can be prevented by vaccinations, which are required by law for dogs.

The breeder you purchased your Corgi from should have started your pup on a vaccination schedule. Make sure your dog has had all of his shots.

Distemper

Distemper is another dangerous disease that has a very low recovery rate. The danger from this very contagious virus is greatest in dogs three to six months of age and in dogs over six years of age. Symptoms include vomiting, coughing, and fever, and death is the usual outcome.

Parvovirus

Parvovirus is another disease that may be fatal, especially if the symptoms include vomiting and bloody diarrhea. There may be a fever, and the dog will be lethargic and depressed. Dogs with mild cases of the disease generally recover, but young puppies are very susceptible and generally do not survive.

Coronavirus

Coronavirus is a highly contagious virus that results in diarrhea for about a week. The diarrhea may be orange-tinged and will have a strong odor. The disease is rarely fatal, but the dog may need to be treated for dehydration.

Hepatitis

Dogs with mild to moderate cases of hepatitis generally have a fever and are lethargic. They may be reluctant to move and have abdominal tenderness and pale mucous membranes. They will usually recover anywhere from one to five days after showing symptoms. In dogs with severe cases, the dog may vomit, have diarrhea, and develop a cough. Sudden death may result. The disease is spread through virus present in feces and urine.

Leptospirosis

Leptospirosis is a bacteria frequently transmitted through urine, especially that of rats and mice. Symptoms include vomiting, fever, and a reluctance to move. There may also be signs of renal failure. Severe cases can be fatal.

Lyme Disease

The deer tick spreads Lyme disease, and symptoms include lethargy, loss of appetite, and lameness. It is treated with antibiotics. Ask your vet if this disease is a problem in your area.

Newborn pups usually do not need to be vaccinated until they are weaned from their mother's milk.

VACCINATION RECOMMENDATIONS

Vaccination recommendations will depend on where you live or what you're doing with your dog. Most boarding kennels require a bordetella, or kennel cough vaccination, and that's a good idea if you're traveling a lot or showing, as kennel cough is highly contagious. Keep in mind that even with a bordetella shot, your dog may still catch kennel cough. There are over one hundred varieties, and the vaccine only protects against a few of those. Kennel cough can be treated with antibiotics and, while any disease is cause for concern, kennel cough is not usually serious.

The trend now is away from giving every dog every shot, just because the vaccine is available. Some people will even have a blood test done to see if the dog really needs an annual booster. Talk to your veterinarian about what is best for your Corgi.

FLEAS AND TICKS

Depending on where you live and the time of year you get your puppy, you may already have encountered fleas or ticks. Fleas are nasty little critters and, if your dog happens to be allergic to flea saliva, they can make your pet miserable. Be aggressive with flea control. If you live in northern areas where winter is a definite season, with lots of cold, you'll have a short break. If you live in a warmer climate, you're facing a year-round battle.

If your dog is scratching and you suspect fleas, turn him over and inspect his stomach, especially toward the back legs where the fur is thinner. Push the hair against the grain. You may see a flea or two scurrying for cover. Or you may not see a flea at all, but you may notice flecks of flea dirt. If you're not sure if what you're looking at is flea dirt or just regular dirt, collect a bit on a white piece of paper or paper towel, and wet it. If it turns reddish, it's flea dirt. If you don't see anything on your dog but still suspect fleas, run a flea comb through your dog's coat. Flea combs have very fine, closely set teeth that can trap fleas. Once you've determined that there are fleas, the war has begun.

Start with the dog. There are many different products on the market, and your veterinarian can help you choose the one best suited for your dog. If your dog is heavily infested, a good bath using a flea-fighting shampoo is an excellent thing to do first. Most vets will suggest a topical preventative. Some last for two weeks while others last for a month.

Daily vacuuming is as effective as any spray in keeping the flea population down in the house. You can cut up a flea collar and put it in the vacuum bag to help kill the fleas. Also, change the vacuum bag frequently, or you'll be supporting a flea colony in the bag. Wash your dog's bed frequently, as that is where most of the flea eggs will accumulate. Combing your dog with a flea comb will also help trap the unwanted guests. A friend of mine with a different breed of dog combs her dog at the door whenever he comes inside and has had success in keeping down the flea population.

Ticks may or may not be a problem in your area. If you take long walks in tall grass or through brush, you are more likely to pick up a tick or two than in a backyard. Deer ticks, which are very small, can spread Lyme disease. Ask your vet if this is a concern in your area, as there is a vaccine for Lyme disease. You can remove ticks gently with tweezers, or put alcohol on them. Never use a cigarette or anything else that will burn. Undoubtedly, this method would get the tick's attention, but you are also apt to burn your dog. If you don't think you can get the tick off properly or just don't want to try, have your vet do it for you. The important thing is to check your

Many dogs are allergic to flea and tick bites. Check your Corgi's coat for these and other parasites when he comes in from playtime.

If your Corgi has a flea or tick problem, there are many topical products that can be used to treat your dog's coat.

dog on a routine basis if ticks are a problem in your area; do not leave them on your dog. Ticks can be hard to find in a Corgi's thick coat, so be patient and thorough.

ALLERGIES

When you're checking your dog for external parasites, also pay attention to his skin. Corgis are not prone to skin problems, but any dog can develop an allergy. Dogs can be allergic to foods, molds, and pollens, just like people. Usually, these allergies cause itchy skin. If the discomfort is seasonal, it's probably "something in the air." If it's continuous, it could be the food. If your dog's reaction is not too severe, you may have the time to try different foods, such as foods with rice as the basic grain instead of corn. If there's a severe reaction, once again, you'll need a trip to the vet. He or she may want to run some tests, or he or she may suggest a food made of one product only. These special diets have just one ingredient, such as duck, and then by gradually adding other foods, you can eventually determine the exact cause of the allergy. It's a lengthy process; fortunately, most dogs don't need to go this route.

If your dog is allergic to flea saliva, he will bite and scratch where a flea has bitten and may do damage to himself if the irritation drives him to continuous biting and scratching at one spot. Whether or not he is allergic, if he is licking or biting at an area for whatever reason, that area can develop into a "hot spot". Hot spots are raw, red, oozy looking spots that can spread and become infected if not treated. I use a triple antibiotic salve on hot spots, and this seems to clear them up. If a hot spot doesn't get better or continues to get larger, check with your veterinarian.

MANGE

Mange is another skin problem to watch for. There are two types of mange, both caused by tiny mites. With Sarcoptic mange, there is intense itching, and with advanced cases, skin lesions and hair loss. It is treated with ivermectin and, externally, with sulfur dips. Revolution™, a monthly flea and tick preventative, is another effective treatment. Treatment usually lasts for three weeks. The dog's bedding should be thoroughly disinfected or thrown away.

Demodectic mange is passed from the mother to the puppies and affects puppies between the ages of three and ten months. With

Your Corgi may be allergic to other things aside from flea and tick bites. Consult your vet about medication that may help to alleviate these allergic reactions.

Regular brushing of your dog's coat will give you the opportunity to examine his skin for any inflammation or irritation.

Demodectic mange, you may notice hair loss around the eyes, lips, or on the forelegs. The dog may also lose hair at the tips of the ears. Demodectic mange doesn't cause the itching that Sarcoptic mange does, and it is usually diagnosed from skin scrapings. A special shampoo may be recommended, and ivermectin is again used. Demodectic mange, if not widespread on the dog's body, may go away on its own. If it spreads beyond small, localized areas, it may need up to a year of treatment.

INTERNAL PARASITES

Internal parasites can be harder to detect than those living on the surface, and that's why a fecal check once or twice a year is so important. Whipworms, hookworms, and roundworms can all be discovered by a fecal check. Heartworms require a blood test, and tapeworm segments are usually evident in the stool and can be seen with the naked eye.

Tapeworms

Tapeworms are the least harmful and the most common of the worms that may infest your dog. Your dog can acquire tapeworms from swallowing a flea, so controlling the flea population is one of the best ways to prevent tapeworms in your dog. Tapeworm segments are visible in the stool and will look like small grains of rice. Check your dog's tool periodically for evidence of tapeworms.

Hookworms

Hookworm eggs are passed in the feces and can live in the soil. They may also be passed from a bitch to her puppies. Instead of maturing, larvae may live in the bitch and then pass to the puppies through the mammary glands. Hookworms feed on the blood of their host and can cause fatal anemia in puppies.

Roundworms

Roundworms also contaminate the soil, and the eggs are very resistant to adverse conditions. They are able to remain in the soil for years. Most puppies are born with these worms because the larvae are able to live in an intermediate host, in this case the bitch, but not infect her. This is why it is necessary to worm young puppies.

Washing your Corgi with a dog-formulated shampoo and warm water will help to keep his coat and skin in good condition.

Even healthy dogs need to periodically be examined by a veterinarian. Your vet will notice something is wrong if he knows what your pup is like when in good health.

Whipworms

Whipworms can cause deep inflammation of the colon. If your dog has periodic bouts of diarrhea with mucus and blood evident, he may have whipworms. Again, contaminated soil is to blame. Once whipworms are in your soil, paving the entire area is about the only way to totally solve the problem. Protect your dog from worms with periodic fecal checks, and use the medicine your veterinarian prescribes to get rid of them.

Heartworms

Heartworm is a deadly parasite that does not show up in fecal checks but requires a blood test to detect. This parasite can kill or incapacitate your dog, and the cure can be almost as bad as the disease. It is much better to prevent it than cure it. Heartworm larvae develop in mosquitoes and are passed to the dog when a mosquito bites him. These larvae move to the chambers of the right side of the dog's heart. There, the worms mature and produce microfilariae, which circulate in the blood until another mosquito ingests them after feeding on the dog. Adult heartworms can completely fill the heart chambers. An infected dog may tire easily and develop a cough. An annual blood test can tell whether any microfilariae are present. Talk to your veterinarian about a monthly heartworm preventative for your dog. Some prevent only heartworms; some also include chemicals that kill other worms, such as hookworms. There is also a shot available that is effective for up to six months.

If your dog does get heartworms, the first step is to get rid of the adult worms. This treatment involves arsenamide injected intravenously twice a day for two or three days. The worms die slowly and are carried to the lungs by the blood stream, where they gradually disintegrate. This type of slow poison is preferred because if the worms were all killed immediately, simultaneous embolism might prove fatal, and even killing them slowly stresses the lungs and may cause permanent damage. Enforced rest for four to six weeks following treatment is usual to help recovery.

POSSIBLE HEALTH PROBLEMS

Corgis, as a breed, are generally healthy. As mentioned earlier, von Willebrand's is a blood disorder they can inherit. Make sure your breeder tested your dog's parents, and ask for the results. Progressive Retinal Atrophy (PRA) seems to be hereditary in Corgis, so your breeder should have tested your dog's parents. If your puppy was not tested before you got him, you may want to have him tested.

Some veterinarians feel that disc problems are common in Corgis, but others don't think they are any more susceptible than any other breed. Corgis may be more at risk because of the combination of short legs and enthusiasm. Jumping off high places can cause a disc injury. If you're playing Frisbee™ with your Corgi, try to keep it low so that your dog is not leaping and twisting. Also, watch your dog's weight. Corgis love to eat, and it's easy for them to gain a pound or two, which can also lead to back problems.

FIRST AID

With regular checkups, vaccinations as required, and a balanced diet, your Corgi should stay healthy for many years. There is always the chance of an accident, however, so be prepared with some basic knowledge of dog first aid. Your local Red Cross may offer a course in pet first aid. If you suspect your dog may have gotten into something poisonous, you can call the National Animal Poison Control Center at 1-800-548-2423. Have your credit card ready, as there is a consulting fee. Or you may call 1-900-680-0000 and the charges will be added to your phone bill.

Keep some basic first-aid supplies on hand. You should have a roll of gauze, some gauze pads, baby aspirin, betadine, a thermometer, tweezers, and your veterinarian's phone number.

If you're traveling with your Corgi, keep an extra towel or two in the car, as well as a small blanket. A blanket can make moving an injured dog easier and safer and should be used to keep him warm if he is in shock. Also think about what you would use as a muzzle if your dog were injured. A dog in pain will snap and bite at anything, even your loving hands. A muzzle will protect you and make it easier to treat and transport your dog. You might consider buying a nylon muzzle from a pet supply store or catalog, or you can use a length of gauze from the roll in the first-aid kit.

To properly apply a muzzle of gauze (or rope or a lead, if necessary), make a loop by tying a half-knot in the gauze. Place the loop over the dog's muzzle with the half-knot on top. This will probably be easier to do if you are behind the dog, and will also lessen the chance of a bite. Tighten the knot, and bring the ends of the gauze under the muzzle. Make another half knot, then bring the ends up behind the dog's ears and tie a bow or other quick-release knot. Now you can examine or transport your Corgi without fear of being bitten.

Never muzzle a dog that is having trouble breathing. If there is danger of a bite, cover the dog's head with a blanket while you are examining him. It may not prevent a bite, but it may help.

If you suspect a broken leg, a magazine or newspaper wrapped around the leg and held in place with gauze will work as a temporary splint. Always run a splint beyond the joints on either side of a break to help stabilize the bone. With any emergency, your first-aid efforts are just that...first aid, a way of quickly dealing with the situation so that you can then get the dog to the veterinarian. If possible, take the extra time to call ahead and alert your veterinarian and his staff to the emergency. They can then be ready for your arrival, and no time will be wasted.

Examine your Pembroke Welsh Corgi carefully for scrapes and bruises when returning in from playtime. Look for burrs or twigs that may become stuck in the pads of the paws.

Household Dangers

There are many household items that may be a threat to your dog. Garden supplies like insecticides and fertilizers may be harmful. Cleaning supplies can be a threat. Antifreeze has a sweet taste to dogs, so they may lick it off the driveway or the floor of the garage. As little as one teaspoon can cause irreversible kidney damage and can be fatal for a small dog. Clean up spills quickly and thoroughly.

Foods that we enjoy may not be so good for that begging Corgi by your side. As little as 1 ounce of unsweetened baking chocolate can be deadly for a small dog. Milk chocolate is not as toxic, but if eaten in a large enough quantity, may make the dog sick or may even be fatal. Foods to watch out for include onions and onion powder, salt, macadamia nuts, cigarettes and cigars, yeast dough, coffee, and tea. Stay-alert (non-drowsy) formulas in certain drugs can cause convulsions in dogs. Ibuprofen can cause kidney damage or gastric ulcers in dogs.

Many plants are toxic to dogs. Ask your nursery for a complete reference on plants you want to purchase. When in doubt, keep the plants well out of your dog's reach. This includes tomato plant stems and leaves and rhubarb leaves.

This doesn't mean that you can't have a garden as well as a dog. For instance, the bulbs of many plants are poisonous, but most Corgis, beyond the puppy stage, will probably not bother digging up bulbs. Keep an eye on the dog, certainly, but don't give up your tulips and daffodils.

Generally, a veterinarian should examine your dog if any problem lasts 24 hours or more, such as vomiting, diarrhea, fever, lack of appetite, and weakness. The longer you have your Corgi, the better you'll be able to tell whether a stomach upset just requires some cooked meat and rice to correct it or whether you need the veterinarian. When in doubt, make the appointment. You'll feel better knowing just what the problem is, and when it comes to your Corgi's health, it really is better to be safe than sorry. Your dog will never need the latest in jogging shoes, will never want a car, and will never need a tuition loan. Don't skimp on his health care.

There may be times when your veterinarian will prescribe some form of medication for your Corgi. Usually, this will be in pill form. If it's an antibiotic, make sure you give it all, even if your dog seems to be better. You want to make sure that an infection is taken care of and doesn't have a chance to flair up again. Pills are probably the

Accidents do happen. Keep an eye on him when he's outside. If your dog should become injured, contact your veterinarian immediately.

easiest form of medicine to give a Corgi. As mentioned earlier, most Corgis are chowhounds. Many will gulp down a pill all by itself or if it's just lying on top of their food. Otherwise, a bit of food around the pill will make it acceptable. With Corgis, this can be just about anything. You can use a spoonful of yogurt, a dab of peanut butter, some cream cheese, a bite of hot dog, some canned dog food, almost anything that your dog will eat quickly, taking the pill with it.

Liquids are a bit harder, unless they have a good flavor and can be mixed with the dog's food. If that doesn't work, pull the dog's lower lip out on the side, making a little pocket into which you can pour the liquid. Then quickly close the dog's mouth and gently stroke his throat until he swallows. Having a helper to hold the dog might be a good idea.

When I've had to put drops and ointment into my Corgi's eye, I've held him between my legs and approached the eye from behind. It's not too hard to gently hold open the eye a bit and squeeze in drops or ointment. With ointments, I then close the eye tightly so that the salve will melt and it won't just stick to the eyelashes.

With scrapes and cuts on the body, most Corgis don't mind your attentions. If it's sensitive or painful, get someone to help you. You may even want to consider a muzzle. The most loving pet may snap if he's hurt.

If your dog has been vomiting or has had diarrhea, he may be dehydrated. My Corgis will eat ice cubes in any weather, so I give those. Chicken or beef bouillon may also tempt them, and the salty taste may encourage them to head for the water bowl, as well. Water drained from a can of tuna fish may flavor a bowl of water enough to encourage your Corgi to drink.

SPAYING AND NEUTERING

Between six months and two years, besides ending the growth period, your dog will become sexually mature. Spaying or neutering can eliminate some of the manifestations of sexually maturity, and certainly this is the best approach if you are not seriously committed to showing or breeding.

As your male matures, he will start "lifting his leg" more and more frequently on walks, marking his territory and announcing his presence to other dogs. He may start marking in the house, as well, which can be a very hard habit to break. He may or may not become more aggressive toward other males. He will certainly

Spaying or neutering your Pembroke Welsh Corgi can help correct some problem behaviors. It can also help your dog live a longer, healthier life.

become more interested in females. If he is around a female in season, he will pay less attention, if any, to you. If he were to ever get loose, he would be more apt to stray farther from home than a neutered male. An intact male may also try to be more assertive with members of the family, so be aware and correct any attempts by your Corgi to "take over."

If you have a female, you can expect her to come in season sometime between six months and a year of age, and then every six to eight months after that. Ask your breeder what the females are like in her line, as there can be some variation. A bitch is in season for about 21 days, although she is only receptive to a male for three to five of those days. The amount of discharge can vary, and how clean she is can also make a difference in how much cleaning up you do. You may want to confine your dog to a room without carpeting while she is in season. If you have a fenced yard and plan to put her out unattended, make sure the fence is solid and is high enough to prevent any wandering males from jumping in. Keep an eye on her. Don't just put her out and forget her. If you are walking her, keep a good grip on the lead and keep your eye out for romantic males. If you own more than one dog and one is an intact male, you just might want to board the bitch, rather than deal with trying to keep her separated from the male in the house. Males can be very persistent and frequently vocal, and three weeks can be a long time.

Neither spaying nor neutering is difficult or particularly hard on a healthy, young dog. Neutering is the easier of the two because the testicles are external. After anesthetizing the animal, an incision is made at the base of the scrotum, the testicles are removed, and the incision is stitched up. Most veterinarians will keep your dog overnight to make sure the dog is completely recovered from the anesthetic, and that's it. Sometimes an owner is worried about appearance, and then the vet will do a vasectomy, which is a bit more complicated.

Spaying takes a little longer because it is abdominal surgery. The dog is anesthetized, and a short incision is made in the abdomen and in the wall of muscle. The doctor draws the ovaries and uterus out, ties off blood vessels, cuts the uterus and ovaries free, pushes the remaining tissue and fat back into the abdomen, and stitches up the incision. Again, the dog will be held overnight. You will need to return to the veterinarian's in about ten days to have the stitches removed. During that time, it is a good idea to keep an eye on the incision just in case. Redness or puffiness could indicate infection.

Besides the benefits of no unwanted litters, spaying a female before her third heat lowers the chance of mammary tumors. After the third heat, there is not much difference in the incidence of these tumors, but spaying does end the chance of pyometra and other reproductive infections as well as the twice-yearly "season."

Intact males may be susceptible to prostatic hypertrophy, which is a benign enlargement of the prostate. Neutering prevents prostate problems and may curb aggression and end marking in the house.

On this last point, if you have had a male that persists in lifting his leg against any and all furniture, it is a real relief when he stops. I showed my male until he was about four, and then considered neutering, but was told that at his age, his behavior patterns were set and neutering would probably not change his habit of marking. For this reason, I left him alone, going through rolls and rolls of paper towels and bottles and bottles of white vinegar. Then I decided to purchase a puppy bitch to show. I wanted no accidental

Before beginning any breeding program, make sure you know exactly what it entails. Lots of time, patience, and money go into each litter of newborn pups.

litters and didn't want the hassle of keeping them separated or boarding one or the other when the bitch came in season. Griffin was neutered. He hasn't marked since. This might not be true for everyone, but it is definitely worth a try.

There shouldn't be much weight gain in a spayed or neutered animal if the exercise level doesn't change. None of my females ever gained any weight after spaying, but my male did, in fact, gain a bit. Cutting his food by about a quarter of a cup brought him back to his ideal weight.

BREEDING

If you bought your puppy as a pet, the breeder probably gave you a limited registration and may have made spaying or neutering a requirement of the purchase. If, however, the breeder sees promise in the dog and agrees that the quality is there for breeding, be aware that breeding is not something to be undertaken lightly. For starters, there's the stud fee and the cost of shipping your bitch to the male. If you decide on chilled or frozen semen, there's expense involved in gathering, shipping, and inseminating. With these last methods, you'll need daily testing to determine when your female is ready to be bred. There'll be testing for brucellosis, as well as for any hereditary problems. There's the cost of an ultrasound to determine the number of puppies. You'll need to buy or build a whelping box. The female may need a caesarian section. Some or all of the puppies could die of various causes. The mother could die, leaving you with an orphan litter to feed and clean every two hours.

If no one wants the puppies, they'll be your responsibility until you do find them a home, and that means vaccinations, worming, crate training, and the beginning of housetraining.

Breeding is not for the faint of heart. If you are not seriously committed to raising and breeding Corgis and just want another pet, go back to your breeder and buy another one. It will be a lot less work, and you'll be much happier.

DENTAL CARE

CHEWING

Corgi puppies are like all puppies everywhere; they love to chew. Chewing feels good when puppies are teething, and depending on what they chew, it also helps keep their teeth clean and their gums healthy. Chewing is also one of the ways puppies learn about their world. Human toddlers and puppies are alike in that they will try to put anything and everything into their mouths.

It's your job to make sure that what they chew on is safe. Also, if you don't want your chair rungs destroyed, holes chewed in your rug, or your kitchen linoleum pulled up, you should supply your puppy with approved chew toys.

TEETHING

If your puppy is teething, cold things will feel good on his sore gums. Wet a washcloth (one you are willing to sacrifice to sharp teeth), put it in a plastic bag, and freeze it. When it's frozen, take it out of the bag and let your puppy chew on it. An ice cube may also make a good teething toy. Keeping nylon bones in the freezer in between chewing sessions will make them more attractive, too. Raw carrots and whole apples make good, safe chew toys as well.

Chew toys help to promote healthy teeth and gums. Give your Corgi a safe chew toy to play with.

Chew Toys and Healthy Teeth

Your Corgi, like all dogs, needs to chew. Chewing is a normal activity and helps to strengthen your dog's teeth. Many chew toys are designed to help clean your dog's teeth as he chews. The Nylabone® Dental Chew has raised tips that rub against the teeth and help to remove plaque. Another veterinarian-recommended product is Nylabone® Dental Chew Floss®, which cleans between the teeth as your dog chews. No matter which chew toys you choose, make sure they are safe for your dog.

PROMOTING DENTAL HEALTH

Start promoting dental health by feeding dry dog food, which will help a little in keeping plaque from forming, although many Corgis barely chew their food at all.

Dog biscuits are another help, as are nylon bones and rawhide bones or strips. The nylon bones get rough ends as they are chewed, acting like a toothbrush, and any small bits of nylon that may be ingested pass harmlessly through the system. Rawhide bones are also good, but require more supervision. Some dogs experience no trouble with rawhide, but other dogs tend to chew off large chunks and swallow them whole. These swallowed chunks can lead to intestinal blockage or stomach upset. Rawhide strips are more likely to cause this kind of a problem than a rawhide bone, but both can cause problems. The rawhide form least likely to cause problems is the pressed rawhide bone, which consists of tiny shavings of rawhide molded into a bone shape. This eliminates the worry of the dog biting off and swallowing large, indigestible chunks.

Rawhide doesn't last as long as the nylon bones, either. While a nylon bone may seem more expensive, it will be cheaper in the long run. Even small dogs like Corgis can demolish large rawhide bones quickly. Also, if you have more than one dog, they are more apt to get into a fight over the rawhide than they are over the nylon bones.

Real bones require the most supervision of all. While a large knucklebone is probably safe for your Corgi to chew, many bones can splinter or will have sharp points that can harm your dog. Swallowing bone shards can lead to serious problems if those pieces should pierce the intestines. Even with smooth bones, if your dog is an aggressive chewer, he can end up with a large mass of indigestible bone in his stomach, which can lead to vomiting or even a blockage in the intestine. Real bones, if given at all, should

Some dog foods help to keep your dog's teeth clean. A harder dog food helps to remove tartar buildup.

be fed outside. They are usually too messy to allow the dog to have on your carpeting. The best idea is to stay away from real bones altogether.

Stringy rope toys can be very effective at cleaning your dog's teeth, but again, supervise your dog while he plays with this kind of a toy. Even puppy Corgis can totally destroy a toy in very little time, and you don't want your dog to swallow the strings, which could cause serious intestinal damage.

More and more pet food manufacturers and pet supply manufacturers are developing different kinds of bones and treats to help prevent dental problems.

Teeth Brushing

Besides providing appropriate chew toys for your dog, you can also help with his dental health by brushing his teeth regularly. There are special brushes for brushing your dog's teeth, as well as smaller plastic "brushes" that fit over your finger. You can also wrap

Hard biscuits are also a good way to keep your Corgi's teeth clean.

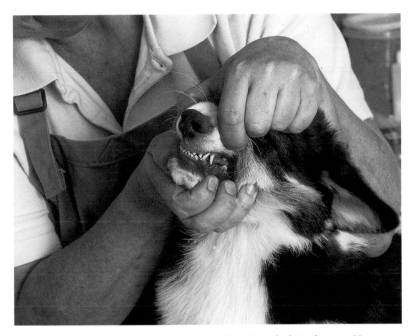

Regular brushing doesn't always keep your Corgi's teeth their cleanest. Have your dog's teeth professionally cleaned to make sure they are their healthiest.

a piece of gauze around your finger and use that to go over the dog's teeth and gently rub the gums. Most veterinarians and pet supply stores also have special pastes for brushing your dog's teeth. These pastes come in flavors like chicken or liver. If you use a paste, make sure it is a paste made especially for dogs; never use human toothpaste on your dog.

Your veterinarian may suggest that you begin to brush your dog's teeth, but if he doesn't mention it, you should. Dental care is as important in dogs as it is in people, and starting young will help to protect your dog's health. Although dogs are not as susceptible to tooth decay as humans, they do develop plaque; if not removed, plaque hardens to tartar. Tartar, in turn, can cause abscesses, and the bacteria from those abscesses can circulate in the system and lead to pneumonia or heart, liver, or kidney problems.

Professional Cleanings

There may come a time when your veterinarian recommends a professional cleaning for your dog's teeth. This entails anesthetizing your dog. The veterinarian or technician then removes any tartar buildup and cleans and polishes your dog's teeth, much like your dentist cleans your own teeth. If any cracked or broken teeth are found, they will be removed at the same time. If there are any abscesses or if there is infection anywhere in the gums, your dog will probably be put on an antibiotic. If your dog is older, the veterinarian may also recommend blood tests before the cleaning to make sure the dog can safely handle the anesthesia. This safeguard is well worth it, and with older dogs, may help your veterinarian detect other health problems as well.

Not all dogs are alike, of course. Some dogs may need their teeth cleaned every six months; some may go their entire lives without needing a professional cleaning. Have your veterinarian check your dog's teeth at least once a year. If you notice that your Corgi's breath smells more than his normal "dog breath," or if he is drooling, pawing at his mouth, or having trouble eating hard food and no longer wants to chew on toys or bones, make an appointment with your veterinarian.

Dental care is easily overlooked, but statistics show that 75 percent of all dogs have some kind of periodontal problem by the time they are four years old. This is why it's so important to include your Corgi's mouth and teeth in every health check

TRAVELING With Your Corgi

T raveling with your Corgi, whether it's a trip to the store or a trip across the country, should be enjoyable for everyone. Most Corgis enjoy a ride in the car, although some may get a bit carsick as puppies. Carry a roll of paper towels with you, and you can easily clean up after the little one. To ensure that your pet will always be a willing traveler, start when he's a puppy to get him used to the car. Take him for short rides that don't always end at the veterinarian's office. How eager would you be to get in the car if you always ended up at the doctor's office? Take the puppy with you when you drop off the kids at school. Load him in the car when you make a quick trip to the bank. Carry him into the bank with you. Most banks keep dog treats on hand, and not only will this be a happy car ride, it's a good way to socialize the puppy at the same time.

Anytime you can take the dog with you, do it. Reward him with treats when he jumps in the car. Soon you'll have a dog that begs to

When traveling with your Corgi, he should always be wearing a collar and leash.

go with you every time you pick up your car keys. A word of warning, though. When the sun is shining, the interior of a closed car can reach dangerously high temperatures very quickly. Never take your dog with you if he's going to have to stay in a closed car for very long. Even in the fall and spring, when the outdoor temperature may seem pleasant, the inside of the car can reach fatally high temperatures if the sun is shining. Parking in the shade may not help because as the sun moves, your car may no longer be in the shade. In addition, windows can't safely be left open very far if your dog is loose in the car; Corgis can get through surprisingly small openings, and they will try. Even if your dog is crated, you might not want your windows all the way down. Think ahead. If there's even a chance that the dog will be left in a hot car, leave him at home.

Dogs don't perspire like people, so they can't take as much heat. A dog perspires by panting, taking in cooler air and having a "heat exchange" in the lungs. In a hot car, the dog is breathing in hotter and hotter air, which makes panting less and less efficient. Stress increases the temperature of the dog, and his panting becomes faster, adding to the problem presented by the hot car. It doesn't take long for the heat to cause severe brain damage or death. Even on an overcast day, a car can warm up considerably, so think ahead. A car in direct sun can reach 101°F inside in about 15 minutes, even with the windows wide open. Temperatures over 100°F can cause fever, heat exhaustion, or death. If you can't open the windows and you're not sure of the shade (and remember, shade moves), leave your dog at home.

Very cold weather can also be a threat. Don't assume that your dog's fur coat will protect him. Although cold weather is less of a threat than heat, a prolonged stay in a cold car may also threaten your dog's health.

All of my Corgis ride in crates in the car, but there are other ways to restrain your dog in the car, including special harnesses that attach to the seat belt. What you use is your choice, but use something. Dogs riding loose in the car can distract the driver. Corgis are small enough to get between the driver's feet and the pedals. In an accident, a Corgi can be seriously injured, and if not injured in the actual crash, may escape from the car into traffic. Even if there's not an accident, Corgis are quick. Open the door for just a minute to run into the store and your Corgi may be right beside you, or out in the middle of the road. Restrain your Corgi for safety.

Putting your dog in the back of a pickup is a very bad idea, but if there's no room in the cab, don't let the dog ride loose in the back. Put him in a crate that is securely fastened to the bed or sides of the truck.

CAR TRIPS

When vacation time rolls around, it will be time to decide if you want to take your Corgi along, board him, or use a pet sitter. If you're driving and you want to have your dog with you, plan ahead. Will the dog be allowed at your destination? Will the dog be allowed at any of the places you may be stopping along the way? If there will be overnight stays at motels, call ahead and make sure your pet will be welcome. Some motels will charge an extra fee for a pet. The fee may or may not be refundable. Some motels will agree to let you bring your dog if he will be crated and if he is never left in the room unattended. Find out what the rules are before you arrive at the motel. The advent of the Internet has made checking out various motels much easier, faster, and less expensive.

Traveling with your Corgi should always be fun as well as safe. In the car, your dog should be in a crate, such as the Nylabone® Fold-Away Pet Carrier.

If you're planning on stopping at attractions during the trip, call ahead to check on those, too. Many large parks have kennel facilities. Otherwise, think about where your dog will be while you're enjoying the water slide. Remember, leaving the dog locked in a hot car is not an option. If your entire vacation is going to be visits to parks and museums, a boarding kennel or pet sitter may be a better idea for your Corgi.

If your travel plans include camping, make sure your campground accepts dogs. Find out the rules *before* you go.

If your dog will be traveling with you, you'll need to pack for him as well as for the family. Take a small first-aid kit. Take water for your dog. If you'll be on the road longer than a few days, mix local water with your dog's water so he gets used to the change gradually. Carry dog food. Unless you're absolutely sure it is a kind you can get at your destination, make sure you carry enough for the entire trip. Suddenly changing foods on top of the stress of traveling can lead to digestive upsets.

You should also make sure your dog is wearing a collar and tags. If you're going to be at your destination for a week or more, you might want to have a tag made with the local phone number on it, or the number of someone who will know how to reach you no matter where you are in your travels. Carry your dog's rabies certificate and proof of vaccinations. If your dog is on any medication at all, take enough to last for the length of the trip. If you give heartworm medicine each month, carry it with you. Do you use a monthly flea preventative? Add that to your bag.

My Corgis' travel bag contains a couple of cheap dog bowls, a couple of toys, dog treats, a long lead for exercise if there's a large open space, and two old sheets for covering the beds in motel rooms. When we're at home, the dogs don't sleep on the beds, but when we travel, they love to jump up and be with us while we're reading or watching television. Rugs can be vacuumed, but bedspreads are not washed after every guest, and dog hairs have a way of working into the threads of a bedspread. Be considerate and spread out a sheet. This also prevents mud and water from being transferred from your Corgi to the bedspread. If you don't want to carry your own, ask the housekeeping staff for a sheet. They'd rather launder an extra sheet or two than have to deal with a hairy bedspread.

I also carry extra towels. Corgis love splashing through puddles, and because they're short, this means that their undersides get as

The Nylabone® Fold-Away Pet Carrier is easy to set up and fold down, making traveling with your dog easier.

dirty as their paws. A few extra towels can protect your car and your clothes. Towels make good beds, too. If you don't want to carry food bowls, a paper plate works just fine and can be thrown away, instead of being washed.

Carry cleanup materials with you at all times, and pick up after your dog. No one, not even another dog lover, wants to step in a mess left by your dog. Pick it up. There are all kinds of products on the market that make this easy. There's even one that fastens onto your dog's lead. With Corgis, a small plastic sandwich bag works just fine. Turn it inside out over your hand, pick up the waste, pull the bag forward over it, twist shut, and deposit in the nearest trash receptacle. There are even some biodegradable bags on the market that may be safely flushed.

I also travel with a lightweight folding crate for each dog. The hard-sided crates stay in the car for travel, and the mesh crates go into the motel room. They're much lighter and easier to carry, especially if you're on the second floor and there's no elevator. A few towels on the floor of the crate make it cozy, and your dog has a safe spot when you're not in the room. Crating your dog in a motel room is a good way to prevent any damage to the room. A piece of plastic under the crate, or at least under the food and water dishes, will cut down on stains from any accidental spills.

If you must leave the dog in the room alone, turn on a radio or television. This will mask noises that might otherwise cause your dog to bark. No one wants to listen to your dog bark while you're out enjoying yourself. My own Corgis are very good about being left alone, but I did have one once who was not so good. She frequently barked when left alone. Our solution was to take her with us when we went out to dinner. Of course, if you have a barker and the weather is hot, dinner will have to be the drive-thru window of a fast food restaurant.

I can't stress enough the need to leave your dog crated in a motel room, but I also know that on rare occasions, there will be a dog that just can't tolerate a crate. If that's the case, put out the "do not disturb" sign. You don't want someone coming to clean your room and letting your dog escape. You also don't want your dog barking or growling at whoever opens the door.

If you're staying more than a night or two, you might also consider tipping the housekeeper at the beginning of your stay rather than at the end. This can make whoever cleans your room a bit happier, or at least a bit more willing to vacuum up those Corgi hairs, and let's face it, there will be Corgi hairs.

AIR TRAVEL

You may, of course, be flying to your vacation destination, and that requires different planning. Every airline is different, and the rules change frequently, so check with your specific carrier so there'll be no surprises. All airlines have limits on when they will fly dogs as cargo, and some may have a limit as to how many they will accept on any given flight.

If your dog will be flying as baggage, you will need an airline-approved crate. Plastic may be a better bet than metal because metal tends to absorb more heat. Tape a label on the crate that lists your destination, your name, address, and telephone number, and the dog's name. You might also want to include your veterinarian's phone number. Make sure there is absorbent bedding in the crate. Freeze water in the water dish so that your dog can either lick the ice or drink the water as the ice melts. This prevents the water supply from spilling all at once. You may also want to run a bungee cord over the door to prevent it from opening if the crate is dropped.

If possible, take your Corgi with you everywhere you go.

133

Check with airline personnel about how and when your dog will be loaded and where and when you can pick him up when the flight lands. Plan your route carefully. Plane transfers will be harder on your dog, especially if the plane heats up or the crate is left on the blacktop in the sun. There is also more of a chance that he can get lost en route. If you are traveling in very hot weather, the airline may refuse to fly your dog at all. The optimal temperature range, and frequently the range the airlines use, is 45°F to 85°F. If it will be colder than 45°F or warmer than 85°F at the originating airport, your destination, or anyplace in between that the plane may land, most airlines will refuse to ship your dog.

If you don't actually see your dog being boarded, ask the gate counter agent to call the ramp to make sure your dog is on board. Pick up the dog promptly at your destination. If you don't get your dog is a reasonable amount of time, ask about it, and ask before your plane has taken off again.

Some Corgis may be small enough for soft carriers that will fit under the seat in the cabin. Airlines generally limit the number of live animals they will allow in the passenger section, and they charge for this service, so make your arrangements ahead of time. Don't just arrive at the airport with your dog in his carrier.

If you've decided that you do want to try to take your dog on the plane with you, make sure he's used to the carrier before the trip. Feed him in the carrier. Take him on short car rides in the carrier. If he's crate trained, you shouldn't have too much trouble, but the soft dog carriers are smaller than crates, so there will be a bit of adjustment necessary. Another point to consider when flying is whether or not there is a quarantine at your destination. Britain used to have a six-month quarantine, which they no longer have if your dog meets certain vaccination requirements. Hawaii's quarantine time has recently been shortened. Know what the regulations are before you arrive at your destination.

BOARDING KENNELS

I love having my Corgis with me, but sometimes I want the freedom to sightsee without having to get back to the dogs to feed or exercise them. I want to stay up late and not have to get out of bed at 6 a.m. to walk the dogs. That's when I make arrangements for my dogs to stay at a boarding kennel. If you do your homework, you should have no qualms about leaving your dog behind at a

If you absolutely cannot take your Corgi with you, you may want to leave him at a boarding kennel. Make sure you thoroughly check out the facilities before leaving your dog anywhere.

kennel. Sure, they'd rather be with you, but they'll be safe and well cared for in a kennel. Besides, Corgis are a resilient breed. Your dog may look pathetic when you leave him at the kennel, but harden your heart and walk away. The odds are good that he'll quickly adjust, and if the kennel operator offers a dog biscuit or two, your Corgi will make a new friend in record time.

This does not mean that you don't still have some work to do before you leave your dog. Visit the kennel ahead of time. Take note of the fencing and the runs. The fencing should be in good repair, with no bent pieces of wire that could snag a dog. The runs should be clean. There may be a doggy odor or the odor of a cleaning product, but it shouldn't smell of urine or feces. There should be water in the runs. If there are dishes in the runs, what do they look like? Are they clean? I prefer a kennel where the walls separating the runs are solid on the bottom to prevent contact between the dogs, but I would not reject a kennel where the runs were separated only by chain-link fencing, if everything else met with my approval. Ask about drop-off and pickup times. For an extra fee, some kennels offer a pickup and delivery service. Do they give baths? Dogs pick up a definite kennel odor with an extended stay at a kennel. I like mine to get a bath and a nail trim before they come home.

Many kennels have an exercise yard where dogs have more room than in their run. If you have more than one dog, this gives them a chance to play together. Ask about the kennel's policy regarding putting strange dogs together. Many dogs get along quite well, but if you don't want your dog socializing with others, or you know your dog doesn't get along with other dogs, tell the operator. It's always better to supply too much information, rather than too little.

Some kennels will also offer extras in the way of individual walks on lead, and possibly basic training. If you have a very active Corgi, a daily walk might be a good idea.

Will the staff give your dog any necessary medications? There may be an extra charge for this. What do they do in an emergency? Most kennels will ask for your veterinarian's name, but in an emergency, they may use one they know or someone closer to the kennel. Tell them your preference. When I board our dogs, I always request that any problem be treated aggressively. I would rather pay a veterinary bill for a false alarm than have something serious overlooked.

Once you've chosen a kennel, it might be a good idea to plan a short practice visit for your dog. Board your dog for a couple of nights. This will give your dog a chance to get to know the kennel and the kennel operator, and your dog will also learn that you will return. Also, the younger your dog is, the more easily he will adapt to a kennel. A dog that is ten or twelve years old the first time he is boarded is not going to adjust as quickly as a young dog.

If you have more than one dog, many kennels will let your dogs share a run, often at a reduced price. If you decide on this option, make sure your dogs will get along together if they are fed in the confined area of a run. Possibly the kennel operator will agree to feeding them separately. Again, find out ahead of time.

You may want to take your dog's crate to put into the run, especially if the runs do not have a solid barrier between them. That way your dog can have a private space, which may help until he adjusts to the kennel. Many people like to take their dog's bed to a kennel, and it's a nice thought. My recommendation is an old blanket you don't care about or several old bath towels. Both of these items can be easily washed, and if the dog destroys them, it's no great loss. I've seen dogs destroy lovely, expensive wicker baskets, as well as beanbag beds and beds stuffed with foam. An anxious dog may be a destructive dog.

While the idea of your dog having his favorite toy with him is a comforting thought, for the most part, dogs in kennels don't play with their toys much. Also, a toy or bone that is fine at home where you are supervising your dog may not be a good idea in a kennel run. Most

You can also decide to leave your Corgis with a pet sitter. Pet sitters come to your home to take care of your dogs.

people who run kennels will remove anything they consider unsafe, but it's your decision. If the toy or bone is questionable, leave it at home.

The kennel will supply the dishes and water pails, so leave yours at home. The kennel owner has probably already chosen a dry food that seems to agree with most dogs. If your dog is on a special diet, or you don't want him to change foods while being boarded, most operators will allow you to supply your own food. Do not expect a discount for this. Food is a very minor part of what you're paying for, and as a former kennel owner, I know that it is much easier to feed everyone the same food, rather than fixing several dogs special meals, especially if that special meal includes dry and canned food, supplements, hard boiled eggs, and other items. I was always willing to do whatever the owner wanted to keep the dog happy and healthy, and most kennel operators feel the same, but to suggest they take less money for more work is not appropriate.

PET SITTERS

Another option is hiring a pet sitter. With a pet sitter, your dog remains in his home. He is familiar with the house and yard and, especially for an older dog, there will be less stress. Pet sitters will come in from two to five times a day, for varying lengths of time. They will walk your dog at your request, or play with the dog for a few minutes. Pet sitters are more expensive than a boarding kennel, but there is the advantage that someone is in and out of your own home, possibly even watering your plants and bringing in your mail, and your dog will be in familiar surroundings. If you have an old dog or a dog with any medical problems, using a pet sitter might be a better choice than a boarding kennel.

As with a boarding kennel, if you want to use a pet sitter, make arrangements before you need to. Talk to sitters about the times you would expect them to visit. Find out how they handle emergencies. Are they willing to give medications? What experience have they had, and with what kinds of dogs? Check references. Once you have settled on a sitter, have them visit your home to meet your dog *before* you go away. Two or three meetings are even better. You want both your dog and the sitter to be comfortable with each other.

No matter what option you choose, keep your dog's health and safety in mind when you're planning your vacation.

IDENTIFICATION and Finding the Lost Dog

As responsible dog owners, we do everything we can to keep our dogs happy, healthy, and safe. If we have a fenced yard, we check it periodically to make sure there are no Corgi-sized holes. If we use a tie-out, we make sure it's not worn or frayed. We walk our dogs on lead in safe areas. But sometimes, this isn't enough. A gate gets left open, a door is left ajar, or a tie-out breaks and our dog is gone. He may slip his collar, or if we're traveling, he may jump from the car before the lead is securely fastened.

Accidents can happen, no matter how hard we try to prevent them, but one thing we can do is make sure that our dogs can be identified as ours should they get beyond our control. There are several forms of identification that can be used, and sometimes it's a good idea to use a combination of these.

COLLAR AND TAGS

The most obvious form of identification is a collar with tags. Each license number and rabies tag number makes it possible for someone who finds your dog to locate you as the owner. Most rabies tags list the veterinarian and his or her phone number, and your city or town office will have a record of your dog's license number. Personalized tags with your name and number can make it even easier for someone to reach you if your dog has been found. Some people go a step further and, when they travel, make up a tag with the name and number of the person they are visiting.

These are all good ideas as far as they go, but collars can come off. Tags may become worn and hard to read. If your dog has been stolen, it's all too easy to discard collar and tags. That's why it's a good idea to have another, permanent way to identify your dog.

TATTOOING

Tattooing is one option. Racing Greyhounds are tattooed for permanent identification. Many people who show their dogs also tattoo. The tattoo may be your social security number or the dog's AKC registration number. My newest puppy was tattooed with the breeder's initials and a number relating to her membership in the Canadian Kennel Club. Tattoos don't take long to do, and they are

Tattooing and microchipping are great methods of identifying your Pembroke Welsh Corgi if he should ever become lost. Your dog should also wear his collar and ID tags at all times.

Make sure your backyard is escape-proof if you allow your Pembroke Welsh Corgis free rein in your yard.

relatively painless. Your veterinarian can tattoo your dog, or, you might find a local kennel club that is holding a tattoo clinic. Some groomers may offer the service. The tattoo may be in the ear, which is fairly visible, but more likely it will be on the inner thigh.

One of the drawbacks to tattooing is that if a person doesn't know where to look for a tattoo and doesn't know how to interpret the number, it isn't going to help much. I have made sure that my veterinarian has Rhiannon's tattoo on record, but I don't think anyone will ever find her tattoo. Short-coated dogs have the advantage here, as their tattoos are less likely to be covered with fur. With a Corgi, a full coat totally hides the tattoo. I'm not even sure anymore which thigh has the tattoo, and she's my dog. Actually, I can find it if I look hard enough, but it is difficult under all that hair. If she were to get lost, no one else would probably find the markings, and it's unlikely that any shelter or veterinarian will shave her inner thighs to look for the tattoo.

MICROCHIPS

The method I prefer for identification purposes is the microchip. This tiny chip is about the size of a grain of rice and is injected under the skin of your dog, between the shoulder blades. A scanner reads

Make sure you have a clear, recent photo of your dog in case he becomes lost.

the chip, which has a number. The registry that supplies the chip has a record of that number. There is more than one registry, and when microchips first became popular, not all scanners read chips from all the registries. Now, most scanners will read all the chips. Veterinary offices and animal shelters have scanners and routinely use them to find the owners of lost dogs.

The AKC offers a Companion Animal Recovery system that uses the HomeAgain™ microchip. The information they have on record, which matches my dogs' chips, includes my name and phone number, an alternate name and number, in my case, my mother, and the name, address, phone number, and fax number of my veterinarian. They provide a form for updating any of the necessary information. If any of my dogs were lost anywhere in the country, as long as they were scanned, we could be reunited.

FINDING THE LOST DOG

No matter what method or methods you use for identification, if your dog should become lost, don't rely on tags, tattoos, or microchips to get your dog back. Be aggressive. Make up posters of your dog. If you've got a scanner, a printer, and a computer, you can

If your dog is found wandering the streets, he may be taken to a shelter. Check your local shelter and others in the area if your Corgi becomes lost.

make your own posters, complete with picture. Otherwise, have the local copy shop make them for you. A sharp black and white image may be better than a color picture that doesn't clearly show your dog. Keep a good photo of your dog on hand in case of emergency. Try to get a picture that shows the dog clearly. Fido may look adorable curled up in a ball amongst the sofa cushions, but will that adorable pose help to bring him home? The next time you've got the camera out for a holiday or birthday, take a few snaps of your dog. If he's got any special markings, try to catch those in the shot.

Take the best picture you have and put it on the poster, along with your phone number. Mention the general area where the dog was lost, for instance, in the vicinity of Green Park, or between Maple and Elm Streets. State the dog's sex. Mention age. It may be more helpful to describe him as "puppy" or "older dog with gray muzzle" than just stating a specific age. If the dog is wearing a collar, mention that, as well as the collar's color. If your photo is in black and white, list the color or colors of your dog. If you have a tri-color Corgi, describe his coat as black, tan, and white rather than just tri-color. Offer a reward, but don't specify the amount on the poster

Go door to door and ask your immediate neighbors to keep an eye out for your dog. Leave them a poster. Put posters on area bulletin boards, in veterinarian's offices, and at local stores. Recruit children. They probably cover more territory on foot than the adults in your neighborhood, and they may be more apt to notice a dog. Don't encourage children to actually try to catch your dog. Ask them to come to you and lead you to the dog, or to tell their parents and have them call you. A lost dog is frequently a frightened dog, and you don't want him chased farther away. You also don't want to run the risk of your dog biting someone out of fear.

Call area veterinary hospitals. There's a chance your dog could have been hit by a car and taken to a veterinarian. Call again.

Check with your local animal shelter. Go in person and look at the dogs. Don't rely on phone calls, and don't rely on having someone at a shelter call you. Leave your name and phone number, of course, but also check in person. Notes can be lost, and shelter personnel may change. Corgis are not as common as

Posting signs and placing an ad in the paper are ways to help you find your lost dog.

such breeds as Golden Retrievers or Cocker Spaniels. The person you talk to may not know what a Corgi is. They may have seen your dog and thought he was a mixed breed. Go look at the dogs that have been picked up as strays at least every other day. Show the staff pictures of your dog.

If there's another shelter 20 or 30 miles away, visit it, too. Dogs, even Corgis, can travel amazing distances. Also, if someone picked up your dog and dropped him off again or lost him, he could end up farther away.

Run an ad in the lost and found column of your local newspaper. Ask your area radio stations to announce that your dog is missing. Many newspapers and radio stations are happy to run these kinds of public service announcements at no charge.

Notify your breeder and check with Corgi rescue. Other Corgi owners can be a helpful resource, and if they see a stray Corgi, they can help you get it back. If your area has a local kennel club, let the people there know, too. Dog people are generally eager to help other dog people, and they're more likely than the general public to know what a Corgi looks like.

BEHAVIOR and Canine Communication

THE HUMAN-ANIMAL BOND

It's not just animal lovers who know how good a pet is for a person. There have been numerous studies documenting the importance of a pet in a person's life. Owning a pet can help lower blood pressure, and pet owners recover more quickly after an illness. Older people who own pets tend to stay more active because they are caring for their animals.

PAWSitive InterAction (www.PAWSitiveInterAction.org) held an education summit in April of 2003 to explore the role pets play in people's lives as they grow older. According to a summary of that conference, Dr. Edward Creagan, a professor at the Mayo Clinic Medical School, has been writing prescriptions for over 30 years that instruct cancer patients to get a pet. Pet ownership can help lower blood pressure, decrease the number of visits to a physician, reduce depression, increase heart attack survival, and decrease loneliness. Seniors with pets have 21-percent fewer physician visits and better coping skills. So-called

Pups that have been well socialized before being placed into homes usually bond easily with their new owners.

"happiness" hormones increase, and stress hormones decrease after quiet interaction with a dog.

If a senior's pet is a dog, besides lowering blood pressure and supplying company, he may keep a senior busy with daily walks. A dog can also add a sense of security to someone living on his or her own. Dogs that are regularly taken to visit the residences of nursing homes can help bring people out of their shells, and children who are ill are less aware of their illness when there's a dog to pet. While many dogs have jobs to do, such as herding, guarding a flock, or retrieving game, many more are pets, supplying companionship to millions of people. A study once reported that 97 percent of all pet owners talked to their pets. It is believed that the other 3 percent were lying.

Dogs seem especially suited to being a best friend to their owners. People and dogs are both social animals. Both species are used to living in communal groups. Dogs, as pack animals, are programmed to follow a strong leader. A human being can easily become that leader. Dogs are experts at reading body language, both in other dogs and in humans. They quickly pick up cues and respond to them. Anyone who's ever had a dog has probably noticed how

Dogs are experts at reading body language, whether it is in other dogs or humans. They quickly will pick up on cues and respond to them.

Talking to your dog in a cheerful tone of voice will let him know that you are pleased with his performance and help him to learn what he should and should not do.

excited the dog gets when his lead is picked up. You don't have to ask the dog if he wants to go for a walk; he already knows that's what you have in mind.

Dogs respond readily to tone of voice as well. You can call your dog all kinds of horrible names, and as long as your voice is soft and sweet, he'll love you. He'll also cringe at the words, "good dog" if you say them gruffly. In fact, dogs seem to be better at understanding humans than humans are at understanding dogs. You don't have to understand a dog's bark to understand a dog. Watch his body posture, and you'll learn volumes.

As with any breed, socialization is vital to producing a happy, well-adjusted Corgi. You won't want to take your Corgi out in public much before he has received all his shots, but you can introduce him to new experiences in your own home. Remember that between eight and ten weeks of age, puppies are easily frightened, and they will remember whatever frightened them unfavorably. You can still introduce new sights and sounds, but do it gradually. Try different objects in the backyard, such as tunnels and ramps. Walk your puppy over different textured surfaces.

Once your puppy has all the needed vaccinations, start taking him out in public. If you don't have children, make sure he meets some children. Explain to the children how to gently pet your puppy. Be very careful if you allow the children to hold your pet. Corgis can wiggle, and you don't want him dropped. Take your puppy to the bank. Most banks have doggy treats, and your pup will learn that meeting strangers is a pleasant experience. Carry your own treats so that willing friends and neighbors can offer a goodie to your dog.

Even if formal obedience is not for you, a puppy class or a class in beginning obedience will get your Corgi used to all kinds of other dogs, as well as people; for an independent thinker like the Corgi, those obedience lessons are going to be a good thing.

Dogs, more than any other animal, seem to gladly work with us and enjoy being with us. Service dogs help make the lives of those with disabilities more enjoyable. Guide dogs for the blind are the example most people think of first, but dogs can also be trained to alert the hard of hearing to common household sounds, pull wheelchairs, open and close doors, turn lights on and off, retrieve various objects (from a dropped coin to a portable telephone), and many more tasks. Once a service dog is trained and placed, the dog frequently learns even more behaviors that fit the lifestyle of his particular owner. Dogs can help people with epilepsy, as well as provide support for people who are unsteady on their feet or who may be subject to dizzy spells.

Search and rescue teams help during disasters, and many police and fire departments have dogs that assist in finding missing persons. Dogs are trained for protection work as well as guard duty, and everyone has heard of drug dogs, trained to find illegal drugs, as well as arson dogs, which can help determine the cause of fires. There are experiments now to see if dogs can detect specific diseases, like cancer.

While bigger dogs may be needed for such tasks as police protection work, Corgis work very well as other kinds of service dogs. Many dogs that help the hearing impaired are Corgis, and Corgis can also help people with epilepsy, getting help when it's needed. For a petite woman who is blind, a Corgi might be a more comfortable choice as a guide dog than a bigger German Shepherd Dog or a Labrador Retriever.

Taking care of a dog is a good way for a child to learn responsibility. A word of caution here: While children can certainly manage many of the chores associated with dog care, depending on their age, an adult should always have the final authority and should make sure that the dog is cared for. It's up to the adult to make sure the dog doesn't go hungry because the child forgot to feed him. It's also up to the adult to take the dog to the veterinarian for necessary care.

Depending on their age, children can make sure the dog's water bowl is always clean and full. They can feed the dog, walk the dog, and brush the dog. Supervise these activities the first few times. Don't let the child tease the dog while feeding him. Even the gentlest dog may growl over food. There are ways to train a dog not to show aggression over food, but part of the responsibility should still be with the child. If your child will be grooming the dog, teach him or her how to be gentle. Unless your child is a teenager, I'd leave fur trimming and nail clipping in the hands of an adult.

The nice thing about a Corgi is that he is small enough for most older children to handle on a walk. Corgis can pull, however, so make sure your dog is trained to walk nicely before turning dog and child loose. I'd also be a bit cautious of whether there were any loose dogs in the neighborhood. Most Corgis do well with other dogs, but males, especially, may be aggressive toward bigger dogs. Make sure you understand your own dog's quirks before letting child and dog go off unattended.

Almost all breeds of dogs were developed to do something. Today, the Rottweiler may never pull a cart, the Beagle may never trail a rabbit, and the Corgi may never herd a cow. It's up to you to give your dog something to do. Dogs, just like people, can get bored, and a Corgi is an intelligent dog that likes to work. You don't need to get a flock of ducks or some sheep or cows to keep your Corgi busy. If you have children, chances are, they'll keep your Corgi active with soccer games, playing fetch, and just running. If you don't have children and aren't interested in obedience or agility, you can still be active with your dog. Besides long walks and playing fetch, there are indoor games you can play that will exercise both your Corgi's body and his mind.

A few lessons in basic obedience will help make living with your Corgi more enjoyable. Even if you aren't interested in formal obedience, every dog should learn the basics of sit, stay, down, and how to walk on a slack lead. It's no fun walking on an icy sidewalk with a Corgi running at the end of the lead. Basic manners should also include not jumping up on guests. Not everyone thinks clothes decorated with muddy paw prints are attractive.

If your dog enjoys stealing the odd sock or two, turn it into a job. As you're loading up the laundry basket, give your Corgi a sock to carry. Ask him to take it or pick it up, or whatever command you choose. Tell him to carry it. Go with him down the stairs or to the laundry room door, and then ask him to leave it in the basket. This will take a bit of guidance, but you'll be surprised at how fast a Corgi will learn this.

Hide-and-seek is a good game, too. Put your dog on a sit-stay. Go to another room. Holler okay. Your dog will eagerly find you and as he learns this game, you can actually hide in a closet or behind a door and he'll find you.

A variation on this game is hiding a treat for your Corgi to find. Keep it simple at first, and then increase the difficulty as your Corgi catches on. This will give your dog some exercise, as well as making him think.

BODY LANGUAGE

Almost everyone knows what a play bow is. When a dog drops to his elbows, with his forequarters down and his hindquarters in

Your Corgi's body language tells a lot about your dog. With a smile on his face and a wag in his tail, this Corgi is anxious to play.

the air, he's inviting another dog—or you—to play. If a dog crouches, or rolls over on his back and looks away, it's a sign of submission. If a dog is standing tall and staring, with ears up and forward, hackles raised, and lips drawn back to show the canine teeth, he is being aggressive. Let's hope your Corgi is never aggressive in your home. If he is, you may need help. It's very rare that a Corgi is aggressive with his family, but if it does happen, get professional help at once.

If a dog's ears are down or back and he is partially crouched and avoiding contact, he is showing fear. A fearful dog may be more dangerous than an aggressive dog. If a dog is afraid and feels he can't escape from whatever he is afraid of, he may bite.

If a dog is showing submissive behavior, he will again avoid eye contact and will most likely roll over on his back. Some submissive dogs will also urinate.

You can steer away from aggressive displays with early socialization and training. If your puppy shows signs of wanting to be dominant, don't play aggressive games, like tug-of-war or wrestling. Hand-feed the puppy, making sure he learns to take the food gently. Don't give him his dinner until he earns it. Even a young dog will quickly learn that he won't get his food until he sits.

If your dog is very submissive, try to give him a little more space. Many dogs eventually grow out of their submissive ways. If your dog seems overly submissive, don't greet him effusively when you arrive home, and don't always bend over him and pet him. Try to have your greetings be a bit calmer.

FEAR

Many aggression problems are based in fear. If a dog is afraid of something and can't escape, or he feels threatened by something, he may respond with growls, snaps, and eventual biting. Physical punishment is not going to help in those kinds of situations. Many dogs that do not live with children are afraid of them. Children move fast, and because they are small, they are frequently at eye level with a dog. Even when they are not, they may stare at a dog, making him feel uncomfortable. A child that suddenly swoops down on a dog and hugs it may be in danger of a bite. The dog may be startled and snap, or he may feel trapped by something he is not familiar with. If a child squeezes too hard or steps on a paw, the dog may bite because of pain.

Yelling at the dog will not help. A dog that is afraid of anything must be gradually taught that there's nothing to be afraid of. In the case of children, every time you and your dog see a child, give your

A dog that shies away from certain people or situations is usually afraid. Properly socialized Corgis should not show fear.

Aggression should never be tolerated in your Corgis. If your dogs are aggressive toward each other, they may eventually be aggressive toward you.

dog a treat. Try to get neighborhood children to help you. Have them stand sideways to the dog and hold still. As you walk near them, treat your dog and speak in a happy tone. Have the child throw treats to the ground as you approach. Don't have the child feed the treat to the dog, bend over, or move at all the first few times you do this. Gradually, the dog can be encouraged to take treats from the child's hand, and eventually, the child should be able to pet the dog.

You need very steady children to make this work, and it's really much better to try to get your puppy used to children early on, rather than have to try to overcome his fear later.

AGGRESSION

In *Pet Behavior Protocols*, Dr. Suzanne Hetts lists several types of aggression and suggests various ways of dealing with them. In all instances, she says that punishment will not cure the problem. It may even make it worse. An example she uses is the scruff shake and the "alpha roll," or forcing your dog onto his back. Far from making the dog submissive, this is more likely to heighten the aggression.

Some dogs become possessive of their homes and bark whenever someone approaches the door. Discourage territorial aggression by redirecting the dog's attention to a toy or a treat.

You run a very real risk of getting bitten when you attempt this kind of control. Fortunately, most Corgis are not dominant aggressive. There are other kinds of aggression a Corgi may display, though, and identifying the cause is necessary before you can deal with the aggression.

For instance, Hetts says aggression may be pain related. If you start to pet your dog and he suddenly snaps when he has never done so before, perhaps he is in pain. Has he hurt his ear or his leg? Is there a possibility of a dental problem? If there seems to be no outside cause for aggression, make an appointment with your veterinarian to rule out physical problems.

A dog may also show aggression over a bone or a favorite toy, or even a stolen sock. Offer to trade him the sock for something better. A yummy piece of chicken may make him forget about the sock. Also, if every time he gives you what he has he gets something better, he will soon be bringing you various objects, hoping for the trade. If your dog is being possessive with another dog in the family, try to let them work it out for themselves first. If actual dog fights result from bones or rawhide, it may be time to eliminate bones and rawhide from the equation.

A dog may exhibit territorial aggression when someone comes to the door and rings the bell. Rather than yelling at the dog, try to redirect his behavior. When the doorbell rings, have him sit and give him a treat. Work with a friend who is willing to keep ringing your doorbell. Put your dog on lead and invite the friend in. Have the dog sit, and have the friend offer a treat. Eventually, your dog will learn that a visitor means good things, and he must sit to get those good things.

Occasionally, there will be a dog that is aggressive for no apparent reason. If you can't figure out what is triggering your dog's aggression or it is getting worse, or you are not, for whatever reason, able to deal with the situation, contact a behaviorist. An aggressive dog is not happy and is a threat to the people around him. Get help before it's too late. Talk to your veterinarian about the problem and ask for a recommendation on whom to contact for help.

MISCHIEF AND MISBEHAVIOR

What people consider mischief or misbehavior may just seem like normal behavior to a dog. A dog that eliminates on your bed when you're away from home is not doing it to "get even" or out of

A mischievous dog can really be a handful. Keep an eye on your dog and pay him lots of attention to get him to stop these behaviors.

spite. He may have gone onto the bed to be comforted by your smell at that location. He may have eliminated because of stress.

Many times, a young dog will "go" indoors after having just been outside. Puppies, especially, can get distracted. They start chasing a leaf, watching a bird, or playing with their human, and they forget what they are really outdoors for. Then they come in, there are no distractions, and they remember that they have to eliminate...and they do. When you are housetraining your puppy, try to prevent any distractions. Take the puppy to the same spot in the yard every time, and wait until he has gone before you start a game or allow him to play.

Puppies that are teething will chew on almost anything. If you've left your good shoes within reach, that will work just as well as a dog toy. It might even seem better, because the shoe will smell like you. The puppy can be close to you and enjoy a good chew. From the puppy's point of view, nothing could be better. If you have a puppy, puppy-proof the house, or make sure the puppy is crated or put into a room where he can't do any damage.

When your Corgi does something that makes you angry, try to look at it from his point of view. Was he stressed? Distracted? Ill? It made you angry, but was it something that the Corgi found enjoyable?

Certainly no one wants their belongings destroyed, no matter what the reason, but if you think ahead, you should be able to prevent most destruction with the help of closed doors and baby gates, or the judicious use of a crate. Even if the occasional chair rung ends up with tooth marks, well, that chair will never provide you with the laughter and love you'll get from your Pembroke Welsh Corgi.

RESOURCES

*Pembroke Welsh Corgi Club of
America, Inc.*
Corresponding Secretary:
Anne Bowes
PO Box 2141
Duxbury, MA 02331-2141
Website: www.pembrokecorgi.org
Email: annebowes@bowesweb.com

American Kennel Club
Headquarters:
260 Madison Avenue
New York, NY 10016

Operations Center:
5580 Centerview Drive
Raleigh, NC 27606-3390

Customer Services:
Phone: (919) 233-9767
Fax: (919) 816-3627
www.akc.org

The Kennel Club
1 Clarges Street
London
W1J 8AB
Phone: 087 0606 6750
Fax: 020 7518 1058
www.the-kennel-club.org.uk

The Canadian Kennel Club
89 Skyway Avenue
Suite 100
Etobicoke, Ontario, Canada
M9W 6R4
Order Desk & Membership:
1-800-250-8040
Fax: (416) 675-6506
www.ckc.ca

The United Kennel Club, Inc.
100 E. Kilgore Road
Kalamazoo, MI 49002-5584
(616) 343-9020
www.ukcdogs.com

INDEX